RAND NATIONAL DEFENSE RESEARCH INSTITUTE

T0170138

A Systematic Process to Facilitate Evidence-Informed Decisionmaking Regarding Program Expansion

The RAND Toolkit, Volume 3

Laurie T. Martin, Coreen Farris, David M. Adamson, Robin M. Weinick

Prepared for the Office of the Secretary of Defense and the Defense Centers of Excellence
for Psychological Health and Traumatic Brain Injury

This research was sponsored by the the Office of the Secretary of Defense (OSD) and the Defense Centers of Excellence for Psychological Health and Traumatic Brain Injury. It was conducted in the Forces and Resources Policy Center, a RAND National Defense Research Institute (NDRI) program. NDRI is a federally funded research and development center sponsored by the OSD, the Joint Staff, the Unified Combatant Commands, the Navy, the Marine Corps, the defense agencies, and the defense Intelligence Community under Contract W74V8H-06-C-0002.

Library of Congress Cataloging-in-Publication Data is available for this publication.

ISBN: 978-0-8330-8417-0

RAND OFFICES
SANTA MONICA, CA • WASHINGTON, DC
PITTSBURGH, PA • NEW ORLEANS, LA • JACKSON, MS • BOSTON, MA
CAMBRIDGE, UK • BRUSSELS, BE
www.rand.org

Preface

Since 2001, the Department of Defense (DoD) has implemented numerous programs designed to enhance psychological health and resilience, as well as improve care and support for service members recovering from traumatic brain injuries (TBI). In this report, we define programs as activities structured to achieve specific objectives over time that are generally driven by broad policy or clinical practice guidelines, and with specific program-related resources such as personnel, financing, and infrastructure.

Despite DoD support of more than 200 psychological health and TBI programs, DoD lacks an approach and process to systematically develop, track, and assess the performance of this portfolio of programs. Further, there is not yet a uniform approach to decisionmaking around program support and expansion of particularly promising, evidence-based programs. This lack of centralized oversight may result in the proliferation of untested programs that are developed without an evidence base; an inefficient use of resources; and added cost and administrative inefficiencies. Further, it raises the potential that some programs—despite the best intentions of their originators—may cause harm or delay entry into the system of care and that such harm would not be identified in a timely fashion.

This report describes a potential model and tools to support a centralized, systematic, and ongoing process by which DoD can make decisions around continued program support and expansion can be made. Note that the focus of these tools is on decisionmaking around program expansion, and does not preclude or address initial funding decisions of particularly promising new programs that may not yet have a solid evidence base. This report includes two tools: a Program Abstraction Form (Appendix A) and the RAND Program Expansion Tool (RPET; Appendix B). The Program Abstraction Form not only collects relevant background information from programs, but also asks explicitly about program effectiveness and the design of the program evaluation used to assess program effectiveness, as a poor evaluation design may lead to incorrect conclusions about the effectiveness of the program.

These tools are designed to support, not supplant, human decisionmaking, and as such do not dictate whether or how a program should be expanded. Such decisions would be made ideally by a representative group of individuals (a decisionmaking board) who serve as the central authority for monitoring such programs and provide decisions about continual program support and potential expansion. We propose a possible model for a decisionmaking board, based on a Human Research Protection Committee. These types of boards, which provide oversight for research studies, a similar model of submission of program information, triage by individuals with expertise in program review and evaluation, and full committee review by the decisionmaking board, may be a useful model for systematically and transparently reviewing the portfolio of DoD programs designed to enhance psychological health and resilience as well as improve care and support for service members recovering from TBIs.

This report is likely to be of interest to decisionmakers within DoD who may use the tools and approaches developed here to foster implementation of a systematic and ongoing process by which DoD can make decisions around continued program support and expansion. The report may also be of use to decisionmakers at the installation or command level who might consider a similar review process. Finally, the report may be useful to program managers who may review the tool to ensure that their program evaluation has the elements of evaluation rigor that the board will assess during the review process.

This research was sponsored by the Office of the Secretary of Defense and the Defense Centers of Excellence for Psychological Health and Traumatic Brain Injury and conducted within the Forces and Resources Policy Center of the RAND National Defense Research Institute, a federally funded research and development center sponsored by the Office of the Secretary of Defense, the Joint Staff, the Unified Combatant Commands, the Navy, the Marine Corps, the defense agencies, and the defense Intelligence Community.

For more information on the RAND Forces and Resources Policy Center, see http://www.rand.org/nsrd/ndri/centers/frp.html or contact the director (contact information is provided on the web page).

Contents

Figures and Tables

Figures

Tables

Summary

Since 2001, the Department of Defense (DoD) has implemented numerous programs to support psychological health and care for traumatic brain injury (TBI) for service members and their families. A variety of factors—including increasing and ongoing awareness regarding the psychological and cognitive consequences of deployment, recommendations resulting from the work of highly visible advisory committees, the expanded numbers of mental health care providers available in military clinical care settings, and the establishment of the Defense Centers of Excellence for Psychological Health and Traumatic Brain Injury—have created significant motivation and momentum for developing such programs. These programs address various components of biological, psychological, social, spiritual, and holistic influences on psychological health along the resilience-prevention-treatment continuum and focus on a variety of clinical and nonclinical concerns.

In 2011, at the request of the Assistant Secretary of Defense for Health Affairs, RAND developed a comprehensive catalog of existing programs sponsored or funded by DoD that enhance psychological health and resilience as well as improve care and support for service members recovering from TBIs. As part of this effort, RAND identified more than 200 programs, defined as activities structured to achieve specific objectives over time that are generally driven by broad policy or clinical practice guidelines, and with specific program-related resources such as personnel, financing, and infrastructure. As part of that effort, RAND developed a series of high-level recommendations for the DoD, identifying areas where efforts may be expanded to better support the needs of service members and their families.

Despite its support of these psychological health and TBI programs, DoD lacks an approach and process to systematically develop, track, and assess the performance of this portfolio of programs. Further, there is not yet a uniform approach to decisionmaking around continued program support and expansion of particularly promising, evidence-based programs. This lack of centralized oversight may result in the proliferation of untested programs that are developed without an evidence base, but with an inefficient use of resources, added cost, and administrative inefficiencies. Further, it raises the potential that some programs—despite the best intentions of their originators—may cause harm or delay entry into the system of care and that such harm would not be identified in a timely fashion. Five specific recommendations were made to address this gap (Weinick et al., 2011):

- The evidence base regarding program effectiveness needs to be developed.
- The evidence base regarding program effectiveness needs to be centralized and made accessible across DoD.
- Programs shown to be ineffective should be discontinued and should not be replicated.

- A central authority should set overall policies and establish guidelines regarding programs, including guidelines governing the proliferation of new programs.
- Both new and existing programs should be tracked on an ongoing basis by a single entity, preferably the same organization that is charged with developing guidance regarding program proliferation.

This report describes a potential model and tools to support a centralized, systematic, and ongoing process by which decisions around program support and expansion can be made.

This report includes two tools: a Program Abstraction Form (Appendix A) and the RAND Program Expansion Tool (RPET; Appendix B). The Program Abstraction Form collects relevant information from programs. In addition to collecting information on program services, population served, and demand for the program, it asks explicitly about program effectiveness (i.e., did the program result in desired outcomes?) and the design of the program evaluation used to assess program effectiveness (a poor evaluation design may lead to incorrect conclusions about the effectiveness of the program).

The RPET was designed for use by a decisionmaking board to systematically assess a candidate program for expansion, based on information provided by the program via the Program Abstraction Form. The RPET addresses four main criteria: quality of evaluation, program effectiveness, priority of the population, and priority of the policy context. Once the RPET is completed by an individual with expertise in program assessment and evaluation, RPET ratings and other program information can be shared with the board. The decisionmaking board can use the information when considering program expansion, using the included decision tree that incorporates key criteria to be considered when making such decisions. Within the decision tree, the quality of the evaluation and the information it provides regarding program effectiveness are prioritized to quickly identify those programs that are not candidates for expansion, or that should be ended due to lack of program effectiveness or—in rare cases—evidence of harm. Information about the priority of the population and the current policy context help to refine maintenance or expansion recommendations.

These tools are designed to support, not supplant, human decisionmaking, and as such do not dictate whether or how a program should be expanded. Such decisions ideally would be made by a well-rounded and representative group of individuals, or decisionmaking board, who serve as the central authority for monitoring such programs, and for decisionmaking around continual program support and potential expansion. We propose a possible model for a decisionmaking board, based on a Human Research Protection Committee, also known as an Institutional Review Board. While these types of boards and committees provide oversight for research studies, a similar model of submission to the board, triage, and full committee review for a subset of programs may provide a useful model for systematically and transparently reviewing the portfolio of DoD programs designed to enhance psychological health and resilience as well as improve care and support for service members recovering from TBIs. Through careful, consistent, and ongoing review of programs, DoD can develop a maximally effective portfolio of programs to support psychological health and services for TBI.

Acknowledgments

We thank Emily Bever who assisted us with the formatting of this report. We also thank Terri Tanielian for her input and helpful suggestions on earlier versions of this draft. We thank our project monitor at the Defense Centers of Excellence for Psychological Health and Traumatic Brain Injury, Col Christopher Robinson, as well as CPT Dayami Liebenguth and Dr. Richard Sechrest, for their support of our work.

We appreciate the comments provided by our reviewers, Matthew Chinman and Ellen Embrey. Their constructive critiques were addressed, as part of RAND's rigorous quality assurance process, to improve the quality of this report.

Abbreviations

DoD	Department of Defense
HRPC	Human Research Protection Committee
RCT	randomized controlled trial
RPET	RAND Program Expansion Tool
TBI	Traumatic Brain Injury

Glossary

- *Comparison Group*: A group of people who did not participate in the program but who have similar characteristics to the people who did (McDavid and Hawthorn, 2006). The performance of people in the comparison group relative to the performance of people who were served by the program helps decisionmakers understand if the program helped people, hurt people, or did not affect them.
- *Effect Size*: The measure of strength of the relationship between two variables (Fergeson, 2009). For a program evaluation, the size of the improvement attributed to the program.
- *Intent-to-Treat Analysis*: An analysis based on the outcomes of everyone who was assigned to participate in a program regardless of whether they completed the program, withdrew, dropped out, or pursued a different option (Fisher et al., 1990). Intent-to-treat analyses are the most conservative strategy by which to account for treatment dropout effects.
- *Nonrandomized controlled trial*: Similar to a randomized controlled trial (RCT) in that individuals who participated in the program are compared to those who did not, but in a nonrandomized controlled trial, the comparison group is a convenience sample (e.g., those with the same condition but not currently enrolled in the program or those participating in another program). Because individuals were not randomized to the comparison group, caution must be used in interpretation of evaluation results, as the two groups may differ in ways that are unrelated to treatment (e.g., severity of condition). However, when data are appropriately analyzed, this design provides useful information on program effectiveness.
- *Pre-Post Design*: In a pre-post design, individuals complete outcome assessments at the start of the program and again at program completion. Each participant's scores are then compared to determine whether they improved on the outcome of interest following program participation. This is a popular and useful design, but again, caution should be used in interpreting the results. Sometimes performance improves over time regardless of program participation, and it can be difficult to determine if improvement is due to the program or some other factor. Similarly, sometimes performance can worsen over time, and this can cause a program to appear unhelpful when it may have prevented participants from getting even worse.
- *Program*: Activities structured to achieve specific objectives over time, generally driven by broad policy or clinical practice guidelines, and with specific program-related resources allocated to it (e.g., personnel, fiscal, infrastructure).
- *Randomized Controlled Trial (RCT)*: An RCT is considered the gold standard for evaluation and is one of the strongest evaluation designs. Individuals are randomly assigned to participate or not participate in the program (e.g., randomized to a wait list or to

receive other services). At the end of the program, the two groups are compared to see if individuals who participated in the program have better outcomes than those who did not. Because individuals were randomly assigned, the two groups should be very similar in terms of sociodemographic characteristics (e.g., percent male, rank). It is reasonable, therefore, to ascribe any observed differences in outcomes to the program. Although an RCT is a strong design, in many cases it is not feasible or ethical, and other evaluation designs will be more practical for evaluating the performance of individual programs.

- *Reliability*: The extent to which measurements are consistent or repeatable (Cohen and Swerdlik, 2002).
- *Representative sample*: A sample of participants in which the characteristics of all program participants are adequately represented (Bordens and Abbott, 1996). For program evaluations, a sample is representative if the people who participated in the evaluation were similar to the people who are served by the program but did not participate in the evaluation.
- *Response Rate*: The number of people who participate in an evaluation divided by the number of people who were invited to participate.
- *Sample*: A relatively small number of individuals drawn from a population for inclusion in a study (Bordens and Abbott, 1996). For program evaluations, the sample is all of the individuals who were included in the evaluation.
- *Selection Bias*: Deviation between the characteristics of people who participated in the evaluation and those who did not (Bordens and Abbott, 1996).
- *Validity*: The extent to which a scale or questionnaire measures the outcome it claims to measure (Cohen and Swerdlik, 2002).

CHAPTER ONE

Introduction

Since 2001, more than 2.2 million service members have been deployed in support of military operations in Iraq and Afghanistan. Although most have coped well with deployment-related stresses, the high operational tempo of the past decade, longer deployments, and frequent redeployments have resulted in significant psychological health problems among service members and their families. To meet the growing need for services to support psychological health and care for traumatic brain injury (TBI), a wide range of programs have been developed and implemented throughout the Department of Defense (DoD) to prevent mental health problems, improve troops' resilience, identify service members experiencing problems and refer them to care, and coordinate or improve mental health services (Weinick et al., 2011). The need for such services is likely to continue despite the drawdown of military activity in Iraq and drawdown of troops in Afghanistan in 2011, since symptoms may emerge or persist for lengthy periods of time.

The growth of programs (defined as activities structured to achieve specific objectives over time that are generally driven by broad policy or clinical practice guidelines, and with specific program-related resources such as personnel, financing, and infrastructure) sometimes occurs rapidly and organically. Programs that address an emergent concern or use a novel technique may grow quickly as decisionmakers in other settings learn about and choose to implement the program. However, a new program that grows quickly may—or may not—be the right program to target for widespread dissemination. Sometimes growth is driven by convincing but untested success stories or through the influence of a charismatic program champion. Without data to inform decisionmaking, ineffective programs may continue to receive support, while highly effective programs may not be able to access sufficient resources to expand their services.

In 2011, RAND published a study that provided a "snapshot" of all programs sponsored or funded by the DoD that supported psychological health and care for TBI (Weinick et al., 2011). The study identified more than 200 separate programs across DoD, the branches of military service, and individual military installations. Findings from that report indicated that less than one-third of DoD programs had been evaluated in the past 12 months.

Among those programs that reported an evaluation of their outcomes, there was considerable variation in the rigor of the evaluation. The main variations included whether the evaluation was conducted by an independent party or by program staff; whether it employed a control group; whether it assessed processes (implementation efforts), outcomes, or both; and the appropriateness of the metrics used. As a result, despite the promise of many of these programs, little is actually known about their effectiveness. Given this wide variation in the quality and strength of evidence for such programs, one recommendation from the RAND study was that DoD develop an infrastructure for regular review of program effectiveness to inform decisionmaking around program support and possible expansion.

A considered approach to program expansion decisions is essential to ensure the well-being of service members and their family members who need care. This highlights a significant need for a process to collect and review information about program effectiveness to support systematic decisions about whether to expand a program or disseminate it to other locations or populations. Such a process could also facilitate the identification of programs in need of additional evidence about the effectiveness of their services, programs that should be discontinued due to their lack of effectiveness, and—in rare cases—programs that may be causing harm.

In the medical field, a strength-of-evidence assessment is a common strategy for examining the effectiveness of a program, intervention, or specific practice. In a typical strength-of-evidence assessment, it is feasible to convene a one-time expert panel or to use structured methods to review the body of available evidence to achieve consensus regarding whether a specific practice is evidence-based and should be widely disseminated. This model is less applicable to DoD-sponsored programs that address psychological health or care for TBI, as the programs may have a limited evidence base (e.g., the program has been implemented at only one location) or may include multiple and continually evolving clinical and nonclinical practices. Furthermore, these programs are situated in a social and political context that contributes to shifting population priorities and funding streams. Often, the state of the evidence is not sufficiently strong to support a long-term recommendation and will need to be regularly reassessed in order to update short-term recommendations.

These constraints necessitate a novel approach to evaluating the extent to which the available body of evidence supports program expansion. RAND's report on DoD-sponsored psychological health and TBI programs recommended two steps to avoid both the proliferation of programs without adequate evidence and duplication of effort across services (Weinick et al., 2011). First, programs supported by DoD should conduct regular program evaluations, and results of these evaluations should be centralized in order to make the evidence base available throughout DoD. Second, decisionmaking regarding program expansion should be systematic and transparent.

The RAND Program Expansion Tool (RPET) tool, described in this report, is one of a set of tools to support ongoing evaluation of the DoD portfolio of programs that address psychological health and TBI. To ensure systematic and transparent decisionmaking regarding program expansion, we developed the following questions for consideration as part of the RPET:

1. Has the program conducted an evaluation?
2. Was the design of the evaluation strong?
3. Was the program effective, ineffective, or harmful? If the program was effective, how large was the effect?
4. What other DoD priorities and contextual factors should be considered?
5. Based on the information in questions 1-4, should program support be withdrawn or reduced, continued at current levels, or expanded?
6. If the program should be expanded, how quickly should expansion proceed? To what new settings or populations should the program be expanded?

The tool is designed to help decisionmakers assess whether a program should be considered for expansion beyond the initial population or setting in which it was developed and first implemented.[1]

The remainder of this report is organized as follows: Chapter Two describes a model and process for establishing a decisionmaking body to review programs, introduces the RPET, and presents four major criteria to guide program expansion decisions. Chapters Three through Five lead the reader through each section of the RPET, describing each of the four evaluation criteria in turn: (1) the quality of program evaluation, (2) program effectiveness, (3) the priority of the population served, and (4) the policy priority. Chapter Six describes the pragmatic and theoretical considerations that policymakers will face as they use the RPET to make decisions around program expansion and dissemination. Appendix A contains the RAND Program Abstraction Form, which provides a standard format for programs to report the results of their evaluations. Appendix B contains the RPET itself, which provides a standard format for reviewers to document the quality of the program evaluation, program effectiveness, and the population and policy priorities relevant to the program. Appendix B also contains the instruction manual for the RAND Program Evaluation Tool.

---

[1] There are a number of existing tools to assess the quality of a program evaluation. However, many of these strategies are designed only to assess randomized control trials or to be used as part of a systematic review of the literature or for more specialized purposes such as guiding a consumer's evaluation of health information. Such existing tools are of limited relevance to the goals of this report, which include the assessment of single, nonpublished, observational studies. After reviewing available quality-assessment tools, we found that none were perfectly suited for a DoD assessment of the quality of evaluations submitted by programs to improve psychological health and the care of TBI. However, two assessment strategies provide a framework to guide the development of the RAND Program Expansion Tool: the data abstraction form for the Guide to Community Preventative Services (Zaza et al., 2000), and the Effective Public Health Practice Project (EPHPP) Quality Assessment Tool for Quantitative Studies (Thomas et al., 2004). The reader interested in a complete analysis of a wider range of quality review tools may wish to consult Deeks et al. (2003); Katrak et al. (2004); or West et al. (2002).

CHAPTER TWO

Assessing Programs for Possible Expansion

As noted in Chapter One, RAND's report on DoD programs that support psychological health and care for TBI recommended creating a single decisionmaking entity within DoD that is charged with regular, ongoing data collection from all relevant programs (Weinick et al., 2011). This chapter describes the potential makeup of this entity, which we will refer to as a decisionmaking board, and a process that this board could follow. The chapter also presents criteria for rating programs and a decision tree for applying these criteria to program expansion decisions.

Program Review Process

Potential Model: Human Research Protection Committee

One potential model for ongoing program reviews is the Human Research Protection Committee (HRPC),[1] also known as an Institutional Review Board, which is often used to review research studies and ensure adequate protections for human subjects participating in a research study. In this model, researchers submit a detailed description of their project to the board using a standardized form. This form includes a number of questions designed to elicit all relevant information that the HRPC needs to make a decision. Once the information is received from the researchers, it is assigned to one or two reviewers who make an initial determination about the project. Some projects meeting specified criteria are considered exempt from review, others may undergo a thorough review by additional members of the HRPC, and some projects may require full committee review. The HRPC may determine that the research has adequate protections and is approved to move forward, or it may request additional information or changes to the research design or protocol and resubmission to the HRPC. To be clear, an HRPC provides an example on which a decisionmaking board could be modeled. It is *not* recommended that an existing HRPC be tasked with the decisionmaking processes outlined in this report. We provide additional information about how such a model may be adapted for program review and expansion decisions.

---

[1] If a Human Research Protection Program includes a Federalwide Assurance, it must have an HRPC within the organization or have a relationship with an external HRPC to review all human subjects research and to grant permission only to those studies that meet ethical guidelines. See U.S. Code of Federal Regulations, Title 45, 2009. RAND has an internal Human Subject Protection Committee, very similar to an HRPC, and the report's authors are familiar with the workings of the process.

Characteristics of a Decisionmaking Board

Although a decisionmaking board may be structured in a number of ways, it is advisable that the board consist of a minimum of eight to ten members with relevant expertise that cuts across multiple domains so that all relevant perspectives may be considered and all services represented. Considerations for selection of board members may include:

- expertise in psychological health
- expertise in care for TBIs
- expertise in program evaluation
- representation from each branch of service
- Veterans Affairs representation related to psychological health and TBI issues
- expertise in DoD program planning and budgeting processes, particularly for the Defense Health Program

Given that the programs under consideration are addressing psychological health and TBI, **it** is strongly recommended that one or more decisionmaking board members have expertise in psychological health and TBI in a military context to ensure that programs are using clinically sound best practices, and to help foster discussions around statistical versus clinical, or "meaningful" significance of program outcomes. Innovation in psychological health, military health care, and implementation of care in response to military operations proceeds at a tempo that cannot be matched by a static decision tool. Therefore, a decisionmaking body must rely instead on the up-to-date expertise of board members to bring additional information—about current operational needs, political realities, and social context—to bear on program expansion decisions. Thus, it is recommended that one or more members have accurate knowledge of DoD resources to support psychological health and the treatment of TBI and be able to reflect on contemporary social and political pressures and priorities.

Program Review Process

- Eight to ten board members
- Board member qualifications may include expertise in:
    - Psychological health
    - TBI
    - Military health
    - Program evaluation
    - Program planning and budgetary processes
- Board meets regularly (e.g., quarterly)
- Review process
    - Each DoD program supporting
        ◦ psychological health or TBI submits
        ◦ a program evaluation to board
    - Individuals with expertise in program evaluation review program, produce initial RPET ratings, triage, and submit programs ready for discussion to the board
    - Full board deliberates on program expansion decision
- Each program periodically reevaluated

Though a single decisionmaking board may be ideal, it may also be more realistic to adopt a tiered system of decisionmaking boards where similar boards exist at the installation level, regional command level, and/or branch of service level. It may not be feasible for one decision-making board to accomplish the necessary program reviews given the sheer number of existing programs and need for regular program review. Further, in some cases, installation or command leaders have initiated programs to meet an identified need for services and have wanted to expand programs without the benefit of a rigorous program review or evaluation. A tiered system of review boards may allow for a more rapid and ongoing review of more localized programs and would allow decisions regarding program support or expansion to be made at the appropriate level. It would also allow for an appeal process for those who wish to challenge a local board's decision to reduce or eliminate a program if they believe the decision was made in error. If this structure is adopted, decisions made by these boards should be shared with the DoD-wide decisionmaking board to ensure that there is a single entity or authority that oversees the full DoD portfolio of programs. Such a tiered structure may also free the DoD-wide decisionmaking board to focus their review efforts on larger programs or those that function in multiple branches of service, as well as those deemed particularly promising (or worrisome) by decisionmaking boards at the lower levels.

It is important to acknowledge that while a single DoD-wide decisionmaking board may provide a necessary central authority to set overall policies and establish guidelines on the review and proliferation of programs, installing such a board with the authority envisioned in this report would represent a major change in operations. Although outside the scope of this report, serious consideration will need to be given to where within the DoD command structure this decisionmaking board would be housed, what kind of authority it would have, how board members are selected or appointed, how long they should serve on the board, and, for a tiered system, ensuring the clear delineation of areas of responsibility and the development of definitive guidance on what programs should be reviewed by which decisionmaking boards and the flow of information across them.

Processes of the Decisionmaking Board

The decisionmaking board would optimally be tasked with decisions about continued (versus withdrawn or reduced) support for existing programs and timing for a greater investment of resources in a promising program. This process, however, is not related to initial funding decisions for new, promising programs. While a similar process may be employed for this purpose, heavier emphasis may need to be placed on policy or population priority, and strong theoretical support or evidence as a promising practice, as these programs will likely not yet have developed a strong evidence base. Developing a process for initial funding of programs is outside the scope of this current report.

To support decisions around program expansion, the board would collect information regularly from programs. We developed the Program Abstraction Form (Appendix A) to provide a standardized method by which programs may report on the design of their program evaluation as well as relevant information about program effectiveness, demand, cost, management, and sustainability.

Once this information has been received, the program would be assigned to one or two reviewers, employed for this purpose and separate from the board, who would use information from the Program Abstraction Form (Appendix A) to complete an initial assessment of the program using the RPET (Appendix B). Given the nuance required to appraise the quality of a program evaluation, it is recommended that the typical reviewer have master's-level training in research and evaluation methodology, have some exposure to statistics and hypothesis testing (e.g., p-values, effect sizes), and be able to identify common problems in evaluation design (e.g., small sample size, nonrepresentative samples). Although the tools described in this report provide guidance to remind the user of key evaluation design considerations, this guidance cannot be used in lieu of appropriate expertise.

The reviewer responsible for reviewing the program would then determine whether the program had conducted an evaluation of sufficient quality, and if so, would present the program summary and preliminary RPET ratings to the full board for review, discussion, and decisionmaking around program support or expansion. When additional information is needed, or when the program had not conducted an evaluation of sufficient quality, the reviewer would report back to the program with recommended next steps and an opportunity to resubmit their information.

The frequency with which the board meets will depend on its workload and design (e.g., one overarching board or a tiered approach; see the previous section, "Characteristics of a Decisionmaking Board"). Initially, the board may meet quarterly or monthly, but as backlog is resolved, it may be necessary to meet only twice yearly. Regardless, the board should meet as often as necessary to ensure continual and ongoing review of programs in a timely manner. As one example, some programs may be asked to submit additional information about program effectiveness; those programs will require an opportunity to resubmit relevant information for the board's consideration in a timely manner. In addition, as programs evolve, the strength of the evidence may grow over time or change in nature (e.g., early evaluations may prove more or less favorable than later efforts). It will be important that the board review programs regularly to ensure that its decisions reflect the *current* state of the evidence for the program (e.g., the board may learn that a promising program that was expanded did not show the same positive impact in a new setting).

Criteria to Guide Program Expansion

Once a decisionmaking board and its processes are in place, an approach is needed to guide decisionmaking about program expansion: which programs to expand, the breadth of expansion, and how quickly to scale up expansion efforts. There are four major criteria to consider when assessing whether a program should be expanded:

- quality of the program evaluation
- program effectiveness
- population priority
- policy priority.

In order to systematically assess these criteria, we developed the RPET to help members of the decisionmaking board to systematically assess a candidate program for expansion. Some RPET questions can be answered based directly on Program Abstraction Form responses provided by the program; other items rely on the expertise and relevant knowledge of the reviewer responsible for the initial review of the program. It should be noted that while the Program Abstraction Form and the RPET are comprehensive, as this process is implemented, both the

Program Abstraction Form and the RPET may be edited or revised to remove or include questions or constructs that the board feels would further improve their decisionmaking process and confidence in their decisions. Each criterion is described in more detail in Chapters Three through Five; the full RPET and RPET Instruction Manual are presented in Appendix B.

After the RPET is completed, the decisionmaking board can use the ratings to make a determination about program expansion. In Figure 2.1, we provide a decision tree to guide such actions. The quality of the evaluation and the information it provides regarding program effectiveness are prioritized to quickly identify those programs that are not candidates for expansion, or that should be ended due to lack of effectiveness or—in rare cases—evidence of harm. Information about the priority of the population and the current policy context help to refine maintenance or expansion recommendations.

Although the RPET was designed to assist in systematic and transparent decisionmaking about program expansion, other factors should also be seriously considered, particularly for those programs where the expansion decision is less clear. These include:

- uniqueness of the program. Is this program unique or are there similar programs in existence?
- fiscal perspective and cost-benefit ratio. Is this program maximizing limited resources? Is it the best use of resources to achieve the desired outcome? Are there other programs that are achieving the same outcomes with fewer resources?
- additional outcomes of interest. Does the program have a positive effect on more than one outcome?
- future need. Is the need for this program expected to increase or decrease over time?
- unique or hard-to-replicate factors that facilitated program success. Are there factors unique to a specific program that facilitated its success?
- availability of materials to support program implementation. To what extent can the program be adapted to meet unique needs of another population or geographic region?
- strength of design. Are there outstanding concerns around the choice of measures, representativeness of the population or comparison group, or other aspects of the evaluation design?
- generalizability. Are similar results likely to be observed in different settings or with different populations?

The above factors influencing such decisions are nuanced and, as a result, the experience and expertise of those tasked with decisionmaking will be vital. Additional information on the decisionmaking process and these relevant considerations regarding program expansion can be found in Chapter Six.

Figure 2.1
Decision Tree

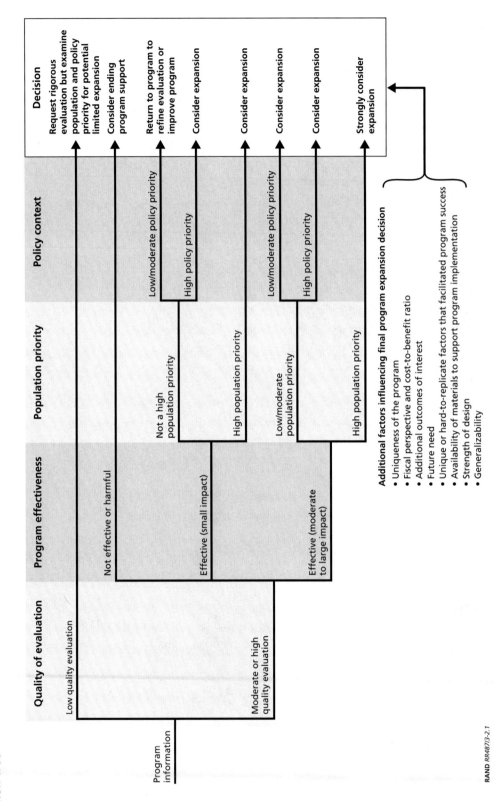

Quality of evaluation

Low quality evaluation

Moderate or high quality evaluation

Program effectiveness

Not effective or harmful

Effective (small impact)

Effective (moderate to large impact)

Population priority

Not a high population priority

High population priority

Low/moderate population priority

High population priority

Policy context

Low/moderate policy priority

High policy priority

Low/moderate policy priority

High policy priority

Decision

Request rigorous evaluation but examine population and policy priority for potential limited expansion

Consider ending program support

Return to program to refine evaluation or improve program

Consider expansion

Consider expansion

Consider expansion

Consider expansion

Strongly consider expansion

Program information

Additional factors influencing final program expansion decision
• Uniqueness of the program
• Fiscal perspective and cost-to-benefit ratio
• Additional outcomes of interest
• Future need
• Unique or hard-to-replicate factors that facilitated program success
• Availability of materials to support program implementation
• Strength of design
• Generalizability

RAND *RR487/3-2.1*

CHAPTER THREE

Quality of Evaluation

Of the four criteria to guide program expansion, the quality of program evaluation(s) conducted to date is perhaps the most important. Without a good quality evaluation, it is difficult, if not impossible, to know whether the program in question is effective and should be considered for expansion. Assessing the quality of any evaluation is thus a necessary first step in determining whether a program ought to be considered for expansion. If a program has not yet conducted an evaluation of its effectiveness, it should be encouraged to do so to ensure that it is producing desired results.

Our approach to rating the quality of evaluation was modeled after the Effective Public Health Practice Project Quality Assessment Tool for Quantitative Studies (Thomas et al., 2004). Each attribute (described in more detail below) is rated by a reviewer as having "low," "moderate," or "high" quality. An attribute receives a "low" rating if design flaws are so significant that the evaluation is not valid. An attribute receives a "high" rating if the evaluation was conducted in accordance with standard recommendations for program evaluation design, and it receives a "moderate" quality rating when the evaluation is not ideal but nonetheless produces interpretable and useful information. While the vast majority of programs will fall clearly within the categories outlined in the RPET, reviewers should note if there are extenuating circumstances that make scoring the program particularly difficult or unique; these issues can then be discussed by the board.

Below we summarize some of the key attributes that should be considered when assessing the quality of a program evaluation. If a program has submitted a Program Abstraction Form (Appendix A) to the board, much of the information necessary to evaluate the quality of the program assessment will be readily available to the reviewer. The reviewer will then use the RPET in conjunction with the instruction manual (Appendix B) to provide a preliminary recommendation. Experienced reviewers may rely solely on the RPET to complete the review, which lists relevant items within the Program Abstraction Form for quick reference by the reviewer. New reviewers may benefit from the detailed instructions, tables to aid decisionmaking, scoring procedures, and rationale for each item described in the accompanying instruction manual.

Selection Bias

Deviation between the characteristics of people who participated in the evaluation and those who did not (Bordens and Abbott, 1996).

Examples

Example 1: Soldiers participate in a resiliency training program predeployment. During deployment, participants complete a questionnaire assessing stress and fatigue.
- **Rating: "Low" quality.** This evaluation design is inadequate to draw conclusions about the effectiveness of the program. The design does not include a group of soldiers who did not attend the program (a comparison group), so it is impossible to know if the soldiers in the program were performing better, the same, or worse than they would have without resiliency training.

Example 2: Soldiers participate in a resiliency training program predeployment. Soldiers who completed the training, as well as a matched sample of soldiers who did not receive the training, complete questionnaires before, during, and after deployment to assess stress and fatigue.
- **Rating: "High" quality.** This evaluation design will allow program staff to examine the effect of the program on stress and fatigue over time relative to a group of similar soldiers who did not receive the training. This design will give program staff confidence that any observed differences between the two groups can be attributed to the effect of the program.

Evaluation Design

Program evaluations are designed to determine whether people who participate in the program are functioning better, the same, or worse than they would have without participating in the program. There are a number of strategies for building this comparison. The best, a randomized controlled trial (RCT, see glossary), rules out many of the confounds that could explain improvement among program participants and increases confidence that any observed improvement is due to the program. However, it is often a costly and difficult type of program evaluation to implement. Thus, most program evaluations will use a research design that balances reductions in the strength of the research design with increased feasibility. The task of the reviewer will be to determine if the balance that was struck preserved a research design that is adequate to allow conclusions to be drawn about the program's performance or if it was so weak that the evaluation's conclusions are invalid and should not be considered. The RPET and instruction manual provide guidance for this task (Appendix B).

Sample Used for the Evaluation

Regardless of the evaluation design, it is important to ensure that the people who are included in a program evaluation are similar to those who are excluded from the evaluation. If they are not similar, any differences between those who are and are not included in the evaluation may bias the evaluation (a phenomenon referred to as selection bias). For example, if individuals with major depression refused to participate in an evaluation of a program designed to improve depressive symptomatology, the evaluation may show more promising results than if such individuals had been included. Alternatively, if those people who are most adversely affected by a

---

Example

A treatment program for posttraumatic stress disorder collects data 12 months after program completion and shows that 85 percent of participants are still symptom free. It claims success even though only 18 percent of individuals agreed to participate in the follow-up survey.

- **Rating: "Low" quality.** This evaluation is flawed as it collects follow-up data only from a small proportion of individuals. No information is available on the symptomatology of the remaining 72 percent of program participants. If they chose not to participate in the follow-up survey for reasons related to the program's services or outcomes (such as feeling that the program did not help them), the survey results could be biased.

---

condition, such as a TBI, drop out of the program, and therefore are not included in the evaluation, selection bias would also be present.

To avoid these problems, programs can take steps to ensure that a high percentage of invited program participants take part in the evaluation, including using a variety of outreach strategies to encourage participation. It is also important to include all types of program participants (e.g., those who complete the full program as well as those who discontinue participation early) so that the evaluation sample is representative of all program participants. The RPET includes a section entitled *Sample Used for the Evaluation* to assess the extent to which the evaluation is based on an appropriate sample of program participants.

Measurement

A well-designed program evaluation determines what the most important program outcomes are and then measures them carefully. The measured outcomes should match the goals outlined in a program's mission statement. If the program's goal is to improve civilian reintegration among service members with TBI, then the evaluation might include employment status, community involvement, and marital satisfaction. It is important to note that while participant satisfaction with the program is an important process measure and can provide insight regarding whether the program was well received, such measures are typically not considered outcomes as they do not measure actual changes in behavior or symptomatology.

If an appropriate program outcome has been selected, the next step is to ensure that the measure used to estimate that outcome has strong psychometric properties. A psychometrically strong measure is *reliable* (it succeeds in measuring the outcome consistently) and *valid* (it succeeds in measuring the outcome it was intended to measure).[1] The RPET includes a section on *Measurement* to assess the extent to which the evaluation utilizes an appropriate outcome variable and measures that outcome appropriately.

---

[1] The RAND Online Measure Repository is a resource that provides information on the content and psychometric quality of relevant questionnaires that can be used to evaluate programs in the areas of psychological health and TBI (Acosta, Reynolds, et al., 2014).

Examples

Example 1: A care coordination program uses satisfaction surveys as a measure of program effectiveness.

- **Rating: "Low" quality.** Here, patient satisfaction surveys provide no assessment of whether service members or their family members have been connected with an appropriate provider and whether they are currently receiving treatment. A better approach would be to measure the number of individuals who had an appropriate provider visit as a result of the care coordination program.

Example 2: A program for service members with major depression asks former participants to "report how they have been doing in the last 12 months."

- **Rating: "Low" quality.** An open-ended question may or may not provide the data necessary to determine if the former participant continues to experience symptoms of depression. A better approach would be to use a reliable and valid measure of major depressive disorder (e.g., the Hamilton Rating Scale for Depression).

CHAPTER FOUR

Program Effectiveness

The second criterion is the program's effectiveness in achieving its intended outcomes. Provided that the quality of the evaluation design is adequate, program effectiveness—the extent to which a program influences the targeted outcome—can be assessed. Using information provided in the Program Abstraction Form about the evaluation design and program's effectiveness, the reviewer rates the program as effective (moderate to large improvement), effective (small improvement), not effective, or harmful. Note that this decision should consider not only statistical significance, but also clinical or "meaningful" improvement. What constitutes a small, moderate, or large improvement is best left to the experts on the decisionmaking board who have substantial knowledge of the outcomes the program is working to influence.

Given the wide range of possible program outcomes and effect sizes, the RPET provides definitions and examples for each rating (see below), but relies on the expertise and subjective judgment of the reviewer to make the final rating. In making this judgment, it is expected that the reviewer will consider the evaluation design and statistical problems that may affect the conclusion. For this reason, it will be important that reviewers are knowledgeable about and comfortable with assessing statistical and evaluation design considerations. Again, while the majority of programs will fit within one of the RPET categories, the reviewer should note any exceptions or qualifications to ratings that should be considered by the decisionmaking board.

Effective (Moderate to Large Improvement)

Some programs improve symptoms, functioning, and attitudes significantly, or may increase resilience and mission readiness noticeably. A moderate or large improvement indicates that the change was large enough that participants note improvements in their quality of life, job performance, resilience, or readiness. Similarly, commanding officers, colleagues, family members, or friends may observe positive changes in participants. Although the final decision regarding program expansion will depend on a variety of factors, programs with this level of

---

Effect Size

The measure of the strength of the relationship between two variables (Fergeson, 2009). For a program evaluation, the size of the improvement attributed to the program.

---

impact are the most likely to receive support from decisionmakers and are good candidates for expansion.

Effective (Small Improvement)

Some programs improve symptoms, functioning, or attitudes, but the improvement is not large enough for participants or others to notice. For example, if a program evaluation found that the incidence of nightmares among those with posttraumatic stress disorder was reduced from 22 to 18 nights per month after participation in the program, the program can be defined as helpful, but may not produce an appreciable gain in quality of life, resilience, or mission readiness. The recommended action regarding program expansion for programs that fall into this category will depend on a variety of factors described in Chapters Five and Six.

Not Effective

Ineffective programs are those that neither improve nor worsen symptoms, functioning, or attitudes. For example, a program with a goal of increasing family resilience that finds similar rates of divorce or marital satisfaction one year post deployment among couples who did and did not participate in the program would be classified as not effective. When considered within a broader context, programs that are not effective may still have negative consequences for service members and their families. If participants invest their time in an ineffective program when they might have otherwise invested their efforts in a program known to improve functioning, their time has been wasted at best, and at worst they may believe they cannot be helped. Similarly, if resources are allocated to an ineffective program that could have been allocated to an effective one, then those shared resources have been invested in a way that reduces the likelihood of positive outcomes that otherwise might have been realized. For these reasons, decisionmakers might choose to withdraw support for ineffective programs.

Programs that are not effective may deserve further examination in two cases, however. First, programs (particularly new ones) may be ineffective due to structural, resource, or fidelity issues that could be easily corrected. In this case, withdrawal of support may prematurely terminate a potentially promising program. Here, DoD may wish to work with the program to identify the specific challenges and to make a plan for rectifying them. Second, programs that are ineffective at meeting stated objectives may be serving important functions within the community or command structure that were not initially intended in the program design. If these community or command-structure outcomes are the true goals of the program, a new evaluation should be conducted that measures the effect of the program on these outcomes and the evaluation should be submitted to the decisionmaking board. Such factors should be considered prior to withdrawing support for ineffective programs and steps taken to work with the program to improve outcomes.

Harmful

Harmful programs are those that, despite the best efforts of program staff, lead to a worsening of symptoms, functioning, or attitudes among those they are designed to help. Although it is often assumed that participation in any program is better than doing without services, this is not always the case and must be tested empirically. To prevent replication or spread of negative outcomes, support for harmful programs should be withdrawn. It is important to note that in some cases, programs previously shown to be helpful may be deemed harmful in a current implementation. For example, a well-known program that is implemented with poor fidelity in a new setting may harm service members.

Board members should be aware that ensuring a program's outcomes remain positive is an ongoing effort that requires continual review as programs are modified and evolve. The decisionmaking board may also wish to reserve the right to audit aggregate, de-identified study data for the purpose of confirming or replicating positive study findings before recommending the program for expansion.

The RPET provides a prompt for the reviewer to rate the effectiveness of the program on the primary and (if applicable) secondary outcome by choosing one of the four options described above. Detailed instructions, tables to aid decisionmaking, and further rationale for including program effectiveness in the RPET can be found in the RPET Instruction Manual (Appendix B).

CHAPTER FIVE

Population and Policy Priorities

The last two criteria include the population and policy priorities. Programs serving high-priority populations and those addressing or responding to major policy priorities may warrant additional consideration in the decisionmaking process. **It is expected that only a very small number of populations and priorities will be rated as high priority.**

Priority of the Population

A population may be considered higher priority if there is an identified need or gap in services for that population or if the population is at particularly high risk for a given outcome. Although the Program Abstraction Form (see Appendix A) will provide some information about the priority of the population, the reviewer should use his or her discretion in rating this criterion, considering only those factors that are sufficiently compelling to influence program expansion decisions. This criterion should be regularly assessed and reevaluated, as a population's priority may change over time as gaps are filled or effective programs are disseminated.

Although all service members are highly valued and can be considered to be a priority population, this criterion will have little usefulness if the majority of programs are rated as such. Rather, this criterion is designed to capture programs serving a population of *exceptionally* high priority. Based on the decision tree (see Figure 2.1 in Chapter Two), when a population is deemed high priority, decisionmakers may accept a lesser quality program for dissemination. Decisionmakers should be certain that a program is designed for a population with a significant unmet need or a population that has been explicitly mandated to receive services through a binding policy recommendation prior to providing a high-priority rating.

Policy Priority

It is also important to review policy priorities, including the current and anticipated future military context, as well as social and political factors that may be relevant to program support. Policy priorities relevant to a program could include a range of factors such as congressional or military mandates, current military actions and deployment cycles, community-level or national support for the program or the issue it is addressing, and civilian or military reports or recommendations related to psychological health or TBI. Careful consideration of external factors relevant to the program expansion and continuation decisions ensures that decisionmaking does not take place in isolation, but rather is responsive to the environment in which those decisions are made. Given that policy priorities can change over time, the reviewer should use discretion and consider only those factors that are sufficiently compelling to influence program expansion decisions.

The RPET provides prompts for the reviewer to evaluate whether the priority of the population and the priority of the policy context are exceptionally high or not. Detailed instructions, tables to aid decisionmaking, and further rationale for can be found in Appendix B.

CHAPTER SIX

Decisionmaking Regarding Program Expansion

Once the RPET has been completed, summary ratings from the tool can be used to support and facilitate DoD decisions around program support and expansion. The RPET was designed to support, not supplant, human decisionmaking and as such does not provide a definitive answer to whether a program should be expanded. Nor does it provide insight into the best approach for expanding promising programs. This chapter addresses two critical questions: (1) "Should the program be expanded or not?" and (2) "If the program should be expanded, then how?" by revisiting the decision tree presented in Chapter Two, discussing a number of additional factors that may bear weight on the final decision, and raising important considerations for the program expansion process.

The Main Decision: Expand the Program or Not?

After the review criteria are applied to programs, the final step involves using RPET ratings to make decisions about program expansion. The decision tree introduced in Chapter Two (Figure 2.1) was developed to help reviewers prioritize the relevant criteria, contributing to a more systematic and transparent decisionmaking process.

Step 1: Assess Quality of Evaluation

The first step is to assess the quality and rigor of the program evaluation that was used to make a determination of program effectiveness. Program evaluations of higher quality give the reviewer more confidence that any observed outcomes were, in fact, due to the program itself.

"Low" quality evaluation. If the quality of the evaluation is deemed to be low based on reviewer ratings in the RPET, the program should be encouraged to conduct a more rigorous evaluation and to submit results of that evaluation to the decisionmaking board. Such information will be important for future consideration of program support or expansion and to ensure that the program is not causing harm.

"Moderate" or "high" quality evaluation. If the quality of the evaluation is deemed to be moderate or high, then the program should be further considered for expansion.

Step 2: Assess Program Effectiveness

Among programs with moderate to strong evaluations, the next step is to consider program effectiveness. Note that this decision should consider not only statistical significance, but also clinical or "meaningful" improvement. What constitutes a small, moderate, or large improvement is best left to the experts on the decisionmaking board who have substantial knowledge of the outcomes the program is working to influence.

Effective. Programs deemed effective (regardless of effect size) should be considered further for expansion.

Not effective or harmful. If an evaluation is sufficiently rigorous and provides adequate evidence that a program is ineffective or is harmful, the program should likely be discontinued. Unfortunately, it is sometimes the case that promising programs are unable to achieve positive outcomes. When this happens, administrators must take action to protect future program participants from direct harm, delays in receiving effective treatment, or loss of confidence in the care they receive. Such actions also ensure that resources can be directed to more effective programs.

Step 3: Assess Priority of Population

Once the quality of an evaluation has been rated as moderate or strong, and the program has provided demonstrable improvements in outcomes, the priority of the population becomes an important consideration.

Not a priority population. When the group targeted by a program is not an exceptionally high-priority population, decisions about program expansion should be based on its success in achieving program goals.

High-priority population. If the group targeted by the program is an exceptionally high-priority population, then the program should be considered for expansion.

Helpful, small effect. If the program was deemed effective but the impact was small, then the decisionmaking body may want to consider expansion. However, given that the program had only a small effect, other factors should be considered to determine whether resources may be better allocated to stronger programs.

Helpful, moderate/large effect. If the program was effective and the impact was moderate or large, then there may be sufficient reason to support program expansion. Programs in this category are not only producing considerable improvements in the quality of life of participants, but are also responsive to community and DoD priorities with respect to the population targeted by the program.

Step 4: Policy Priority

The last decision point takes into account the external context within which the program operates.

Compelling policy factors are present. If there are clear policy priorities that support program expansion (e.g., filling a gap identified in a national task force report), expansion should be considered. However, the strength of that recommendation depends on the effectiveness of the program.

Program impact is small. The decisionmaking body should consider expansion but carefully weigh other factors that may affect expansion decisions.

Program impact is moderate/large. Given the combination of compelling factors (e.g., "high" quality evaluation, moderate/large impact, high policy priority), there may be sufficient reason to support program expansion.

No compelling policy factors. When there are no policy factors that might reasonably influence the recommendations of a decisionmaking body, then the recommendation will largely depend on the magnitude of the program outcome.

Program impact is small. When a program that does not address a population or policy priority reports success on a limited scale, there are few compelling reasons to consider expanding or scaling up the program. At the same time, in light of some demonstrated success, there is likely no cause for discontinuing the program. In this case, a possible recommendation is to continue program support at current levels, but request that the program investigate strategies to improve program outcomes. Programs that receive this recommendation can be encouraged to reference the RAND report *A Program Manager's Guide for Program Improvement in Ongoing Psychological Health and Traumatic Brain Injury Programs: The RAND Toolkit, Volume 4* for guidance (Ryan et al., 2014). Alternatively, as part of their evaluation, the program might examine whether certain individuals derive more benefit from program services than others. If the program is effective for some but not others, the program may consider refining the eligibility criteria for programs services to include only those individuals who are likely to benefit most from services.

Program impact is moderate or large. Given the mix of criteria supporting expansion (quality evaluation, moderate/large effect) and criteria not supporting expansion (not a population or policy priority), the decisionmaking body may still consider program expansion. However, additional factors and competing priorities relevant to the decision should be considered.

Additional Factors to Consider

As part of the decisionmaking process outlined above, additional factors should be considered, particularly for those programs where the expansion decision is less clear. Although these factors are not instantiated in the decision tool, they are important to the final decision and should be considered in conjunction with other material. Given that many of these factors evaluate the target program relative to other programs within the DoD portfolio, this process will not be the responsibility solely of the individual reviewer. Rather, the following topics are factors that the full decisionmaking board should consider prior to making a final recommendation.

Uniqueness of the program. Examined in isolation, a program may appear to be a strong candidate for expansion. However, it is important to consider the universe of similar programs and their potential for overlap. Expanding a program into an area where a similar program already exists is not likely to yield results that are as strong as those of the original program. It may be useful to compare similar programs in an effort to ensure that the most effective programs are supported and sustained, and those that are less effective are either replaced or merged with the more effective program.

Fiscal perspective and cost-to-benefit ratio. Given the limited availability of funding and other resources, decisionmakers examining a program should consider whether there are other programs achieving the same or better results with fewer resources. Even a program with strong positive outcomes may not be a good candidate for expansion if an equally effective, low-cost alternative is already widely disseminated. Given that programs may have multiple components or serve several populations, a given program may be able to expand in specific ways to better meet the needs of an underserved population. Strategic investment decisions may result in greater benefit at a smaller cost than if the full program were expanded.

Additional outcomes of interest. Programs typically have one main outcome of interest. However, large programs may have a number of secondary outcomes that provide additional insight into program effectiveness (e.g., a program whose goal is to reduce symptoms of depression [primary outcome] may also improve related outcomes such as parent-child interactions [secondary outcome]). Decisionmakers may use additional information about the effectiveness of the programs on the range of outcomes to inform decisions regarding expansion. The decisionmaking body may capitalize on this opportunity to assess the extent to which the program is meeting or exceeding its goals for each of these outcomes. If the program is less effective for some outcomes, the recommendation may be that funding for those activities should be reallocated to support expansion of the activities that are showing more promise.

Future need. Projected increases or decreases in need, as well as information on current unmet need, may also inform expansion decisions. For example, if most individuals who want program services are already receiving them, expanding the program may not be recommended, even if the program is yielding impressive results. If the program is already widely available, a needs assessment may be conducted to determine the extent to which the need exists to further spread the program. If the need is small, decisionmakers may wish to either sustain the current level of support or support the development of program capabilities to deliver services to those few still in need. Alternatively, if a needs assessment indicates a significant gap in services in specific areas or populations, or if decisionmakers are aware of future deployment or other military activity that may increase the need for the program, decisionmakers may consider expanding the program to those high-priority areas.

Unique or hard-to-replicate factors that facilitated program success. Another factor for consideration, and perhaps the most difficult to assess, is the extent to which there are unique or hard-to-replicate factors that are instrumental to the program's success. In our assessment of DoD programs that support psychological health and services for TBI, a number of programs noted the importance of in-kind resources, centrally located office space, senior military official buy-in, and on-the-ground program champions for ensuring the program's success (Weinick et al., 2011). In these cases, it is not clear whether replicating the program in another location would yield similar results. Thus, it may be wise to replicate some programs on a smaller scale to first assess whether results similar to the original effort can be achieved prior to scaling the program more broadly.

Availability of materials to support program implementation. In the field of prevention science, there is a recognition that a "curriculum in a box" is not only inappropriate for addressing diverse demographic and contextual characteristics in a community, but that it is unrealistic to assume that a program will be implemented in exactly the same manner across communities. Recent efforts have focused on developing models with core components or elements that can be implemented uniformly, while still allowing for local adaptation (Beckett, Hawken, and Jacknowitz, 2001; Botvin, 2003). Information on which program elements should be considered core components, as well as the availability of program manuals and lessons learned from the implementation of the original program, may help to maximize the likelihood that the program will have the intended effect in the new location. The availability of such materials may influence decisionmaking regarding program expansion.

Strength of design. Though the Program Abstraction Form and the RPET are designed to assess the strength of the evaluation design, there are likely nuances of the evaluation design that should be considered and discussed to determine whether the design was adequate to draw accurate conclusions about the program's effectiveness. This may also include the design of the evaluation itself (e.g., use of a weaker design), choice of measures selected and the psychometric properties of those measures, how well certain outcomes were measured, and the appropriateness of the population selected as well as the comparison group used.

Generalizability. A final factor for consideration is generalizability, or the extent to which evaluation findings may be extended to other populations. Differences across regions and armed services, for example, may produce inequities in program effectiveness across sites. Before expanding a program, it is critical to think about whether similar effects are expected if the program were implemented in a different setting or with a different population.

If the Program Should Be Expanded, Then How?

Once a program is considered a candidate for expansion, the next question facing decision-makers is how best to implement this expansion. Consideration should be paid not only to the extent of the expansion, but also to whether the program should be replicated outright or adapted to suit new locations, conditions, or populations.

Extent of Program Expansion

Although we have characterized the decision regarding program expansion as a yes/no choice, it is designed to be a starting point for a richer and more nuanced discussion of how best to expand a given program. It should be noted that effectively expanding a program in a way that replicates the positive outcomes produced by the original program is a complex and difficult undertaking. We discuss a range of expansion approaches, highlighting situations in which each approach would be useful. A detailed discussion of each is beyond the scope of this report, and interested readers should consult Norton and Mittman (2010) for a comprehensive coverage of scaling decisions.

Within-program expansion. In some cases, an effective program may be operating at full capacity with long wait lists. In this case, it may make more sense to invest resources in expanding the program within the existing location (e.g., hiring additional staff, adding training opportunities), rather than using those resources to replicate the program at another location. This is a relatively low-cost program expansion as it does not involve significant resources for start-up and fulfills an immediate need of an identified population.

Small-scale expansion. Small-scale expansion may be warranted for programs that have demonstrated success in a single location. In these instances, the next step may be to disseminate the program to another location or two and assess whether the program is equally effective in these new contexts before committing to a large-scale expansion. Small-scale expansions may also be warranted for programs that address a unique condition or population. In these cases, decisionmakers may wish to expand the program only to those areas where there is high demand.

Large-scale expansion. Large-scale expansion (e.g., throughout a branch of service or DoD-wide) ideally should be implemented only after a program has demonstrated consistently positive outcomes in a number of settings. Given the logistical challenges of implementing a large-scale expansion of a program, more attention may need to be paid to additional factors such as whether the program has standardized manuals and training procedures to ensure fidelity to its core components.

Replication or Adaptation?

One of the last considerations for program expansion is the extent to which the program slated for expansion should be replicated or adapted.

Replication. To maximize the likelihood of success at a new location, newly implemented programs should replicate as much of the original program as possible. This includes the program procedures and activities, population served, and program staffing model.

Adaptation to new location. In some cases, replication of a program may not be feasible, and elements of the program will need to be adapted to be responsive to the local context and needs of the population. In these cases, caution is warranted. When adaptation is significant, new program evaluation efforts must ensure that previously demonstrated effectiveness is maintained despite changes to the curriculum or procedures.

Adaptation of program to address a new condition or population. An effective program may adapt or expand its services to address a condition or population it has not traditionally served. For example, a program designed to improve family functioning by working with the service member and spouse may choose to expand and adapt its materials for children. Adaptations such as these are best expanded on a very small scale followed by a new program evaluation to ensure that the adapted program is helpful for the newly targeted population.

Conclusion

This report describes a framework and tools to support the development of an ongoing, transparent, and systematic approach to decisionmaking around program expansion. The RPET was designed to help a decisionmaking board consider and prioritize criteria relevant to the decisionmaking process, but does not provide absolute recommendations on whether programs should be expanded. The broad array of programs, populations served, military, policy priorities, and other contextual factors imply the need for the judgment of the decisionmaking board to influence the final determination. It is expected that as the Program Abstraction Form and RPET are implemented, the board may wish to refine the tools to ensure that necessary information is fully captured and important criteria are incorporated into the process. Through careful, consistent, and ongoing review of programs, the DoD can develop a maximally effective portfolio of programs to support psychological health and services for TBI.

Program Abstraction Form

Obtaining relevant and complete data from programs is critical in order to evaluate each program's effectiveness and the quality of any evaluation that has been conducted. To facilitate this process, we developed the Program Abstraction Form to provide a standardized method by which programs may report their efforts and outcomes. Provided that a program can be evaluated and has evaluated its efforts, program staff should be able to address all components included in the Program Abstraction Form. The form could be submitted to an appropriate decisionmaking board for determination of program maintenance or expansion (see Chapter Two).

Section I: Program Description

The first section of the Program Abstraction Form asks for a general description of the program, including program size, mission and goals, and the impetus for or rationale supporting the program. This section also provides a means to collect standardized information about the population served by the program, including the branch or component of service, the percentage of eligible participants currently served by the program, whether there is a waiting list for participation in the program, and the percentage of individuals who withdrew from the program or declined further services. The section also asks about the broad domains that the program addresses (e.g., psychological, social), the specific areas of psychological health or TBI addressed by the program, the program's activities, the mode of service delivery, and the intensity of program services. Responses to these questions will promote a richer understanding of the program by the decisionmaking board and will help to inform the RPET rating of the population and policy priorities relevant to the program (Appendix B).

The Program Abstraction Form is similar in some ways to the RAND Program Classification Tool (Acosta, Gonzalez, et al., 2014). The purpose of the RAND Program Classification Tool is to provide a simple, user-friendly, high-level summary that can be used to describe, catalogue, and compare programs within the DoD portfolio. The Program Abstraction Form, in contrast, facilitates a more detailed look at each program, assessing additional criteria and at a level of detail necessary to inform decisionmaking regarding program expansion. As an example, items 20–22 of the Program Abstraction Form ask specifically about whether the program has a waitlist or is running at full capacity. Such information provides insight on whether expansion of the existing program may be warranted before consideration of other program expansion strategies (such as expansion to new populations). Materials that programs append to their Program Abstraction Form (e.g., manuals) may also be informative, providing evidence of standardized program materials necessary for program expansion.

Section II: Program Evaluation and Effectiveness

The second section facilitates the collection of information needed to evaluate the quality of the evaluation and program effectiveness. This includes the design of the evaluation, including when data were collected, whether a comparison group was used, and response rate (the percentage of those selected to take part in the evaluation who agreed to participate) at baseline and follow-up. Programs are also asked to report on characteristics of the sample used for the evaluation compared to (1) those in the program overall, (2) those eligible for the program but not participating in it, and (3) any comparison group used for the evaluation. Information on how program success was defined and measured is also requested, including information on the psychometric properties of the measures themselves. Finally, information on program effectiveness is collected for up to three outcomes.

Program Abstraction Form

This form supports the systematic collection of information on programs that enhance psychological health and resilience as well as improve care and support for service members recovering from traumatic brain injuries (TBI). The first section focuses on an overall description of your program, including questions about the population you serve. The second section focuses on any evaluation or program assessments that you have completed, either on your own or in partnership with another organization (e.g., university, research organization). Program managers or directors who are unfamiliar with evaluation design and statistics may wish to seek guidance to respond to Section II. Please be as clear and complete as possible in your responses.

Section I: Program Description

1. Date this form was completed _____

2. Program name _____

3. Program oversight (e.g., branch of service and where program is housed within that branch) _____
_____
_____
_____

4. Program director and contact information _____
_____
_____
_____

5. Month and year program was started _____

6. What are the mission and goals of the program? _____
    _____
    _____
    _____
    _____

7. What was the impetus for or rationale behind the development of the program? (e.g.,
    unmet need, congressional mandate)? _____
    _____
    _____
    _____

8. If applicable, describe the theoretical model of the program (i.e., what is the mechanism
    by which participants are helped)? _____
    _____
    _____
    _____
    _____

9. What domains of psychological health and/or traumatic brain injury are addressed by
    the program? (select all that apply)
    - Biological
    - Psychological
    - Social
    - Spiritual
    - Holistic
    - Other (specify) _____

10. What approaches were employed by the programs to address the above domains (select
    all that apply)?
    - Clinical
    - Education/training
    - Prevention/resilience
    - Outreach

11. What specific areas of psychological health and/or traumatic brain injury does the program focus on? (select all that apply)
    ○ Deployment-related issues
    ○ Depression
    ○ Domestic violence
    ○ Families and/or children
    ○ General psychological health
    ○ Improving relationships
    ○ Legal issues
    ○ Postdeployment issues and reintegration
    ○ Posttraumatic stress disorder
    ○ Resilience
    ○ Spiritual issues
    ○ Stress reduction
    ○ Substance use
    ○ Suicide prevention
    ○ Traumatic brain injury
    ○ Other: (specify)_____

12. Where does this program fall on the Continuum of Care for Psychological Health and TBI?
    ○ Prevention
    ○ Surveillance
    ○ Screening
    ○ Diagnosis
    ○ Treatment
    ○ Rehabilitation
    ○ Reintegration

13. What phase(s) of deployment does this program address? (select all that apply)
    ○ Predeployment
    ○ Deployment
    ○ Return or Redeployment
    ○ Postdeployment
    ○ Not related to deployment phase

14. Describe the services provided by your program. Please specify, where applicable, information about the qualifications of individuals providing each service (e.g., training, education). If staff qualifications are less than the program's ideal, please explain (e.g., temporary replacement, staff turnover). Additional materials to describe program services may be appended. _____
    _____
    _____
    _____
    _____

15. Describe the intensity of program services. Specify how often and for how long individuals participate in your program (e.g., meet with counselor once a week for one hour over a six-month period). Additional materials to describe program services may be appended. _____

_____

_____

_____

_____

_____

16. What is the setting or mode of service delivery? (select all that apply)
    ○ Phone
    ○ Face-to-face individual
    ○ Face-to-face group
    ○ Internet
    ○ Outreach/educational material distribution
    ○ Classroom
    ○ Video teleconference
    ○ Other (specify) _____

17. Are services provided on base, off base, or both?
    ○ On base
    ○ Off base
    ○ Both

18. Describe the population served. For each population selected, provide information about eligibility requirements. For example, a program may support service members, but require that they be deploying within the next 30 days to be eligible for program services.
    ○ Service members _____

    _____

    ○ Veterans _____

    _____

    ○ Civilians_____

    _____

    ○ Family members _____

    _____

    _____

    ○ Other (Specify) _____

    _____

    _____

19. What service/component is served by the program? (select all that apply)
    ◦ Department of Defense–wide
    ◦ Department of Veterans Affairs
    ◦ Army
    ◦ Army Reserve
    ◦ Army National Guard
    ◦ Air Force
    ◦ Air Force Reserve
    ◦ Air Guard
    ◦ Navy
    ◦ Navy Reserve
    ◦ Marine Corps
    ◦ Marine Corps Reserve
    ◦ Installation-specific (specify) _____

    _____

20. What is the size of your program? Provide the average number served in the past month, and total number served in the past year.
    Service members _____ per month or _____ per year
    Family members _____ per month or _____ per year
    Other   _____ per month or _____ per year
    TOTAL _____ **per month or** _____ **per year**

20a. Compared to the previous year, this is an
    ◦ increase
    ◦ decrease
    ◦ no change

21. Of the number listed above, how many of the people served by the program in the past year withdrew or declined further services prior to completion of the program?
    People _____
    ◦ Exact number
    ◦ Estimated number

22. What percent of people served by the program withdrew or declined further services prior to completion of the program?
    _____ %
    ◦ Exact number
    ◦ Estimated number

    Calculation Tip: *Q.21 Percent = 100 x Q20 / Q.19TOTAL per year*

23. Does the program have a waiting list?
    ◦ No
    ◦ Yes (How many people are currently on the waiting list? _____)

24. If the program had additional resources to support an expansion (e.g., hire more staff, increase infrastructure), are there additional people in the community the program would be able to serve?
    ◦ No
    ◦ Yes (How many people? _____)
    ◦ Exact number
    ◦ Estimated number

25. Of the people who would be eligible to receive program services, what percentage are currently served by the program?
    _____ %
    ◦ Exact number
    ◦ Estimated number

Calculation Tip: *Q.24 Percent = 100 x Q.19 TOTAL per year / (Q19 TOTAL per year + Q.23)*

26. What is the annual cost of running your program? _____

Section II: Program Evaluation and Effectiveness
In this section, you are asked to provide information on the most recent evaluation that you or someone else conducted on your program. For this section, we use the term *evaluation* to refer to external evaluations conducted by an outside group (e.g., university, research group), as well as self-evaluations or self-assessments conducted by program staff.

27. Has an evaluation been conducted to document the program's effectiveness?
    ◦ No (If no, skip to question 38)
    ◦ Yes, we conducted a self-assessment or self-evaluation
    ◦ Yes, someone else conducted an evaluation of our program

28. When was the evaluation conducted? Please provide date(s) when data were collected, not when data were analyzed. _____
    _____
    _____

29. How many program participants were included in the evaluation (provide both number and percentage of eligible population):
    _____ ___ Exact number ___ Estimated number
    _____% ___ Exact percent ___ Estimated percent

30. Please describe the sampling frame used for this evaluation. _____
    _____
    _____

31. Of the individuals who were selected to take part in the evaluation, what percentage were included in the evaluation? (include all measures collected at any baseline assessment)

- At baseline (the start of their program participation)   _____% or NA
- At the end of their program participation   _____% or NA
- First follow-up data collection   _____% or NA
- Second follow-up data collection   _____% or NA
- Third follow-up data collection   _____% or NA

32. Please provide data on the characteristics of (a) the people who participated in the evaluation and (b) the program population overall. Where possible, please note if there were statistically significant differences between the two groups. An example of a table is provided below. Revise and expand this table as necessary.

	People in the evaluation	All program participants	Are the two groups significantly different? ($p < 0.05$)
Female (%)			
Rank (in categories)			
Baseline measures (average and standard deviation; include all measures collected at any baseline assessment)			
Deployment in past 6 months (%)			

Outcome Measurement

33. How did you measure program success? (select all that apply)
- Questionnaire/scale
- Resource utilization (e.g., number of doctor visits)
- Observation
- Interview
- Laboratory test
- Record review (e.g., medical records)
- Program graduation or completion
- Other _____

34. How is program success defined for this evaluation? Describe in detail and please include information regarding specific effect sizes that you feel constitute success in meeting your program objectives. Where necessary, specify which outcomes are primary, secondary, and tertiary. (*NOTE: Participant satisfaction with the program is a process measure. Do not include participant satisfaction here. Examples of outcomes include a decline in symptoms, improved knowledge about a topic, scheduling an appointment with a mental health provider, or improved resilience.*) _____

_____

_____

_____

_____

_____

35. For each measurement strategy selected in question 33, when applicable, please provide: (a) the name and reference for the selected measure, and (b) any known psychometric properties of the measure. Please append copies of these measures and any supporting documentation on the psychometric properties of the measures to this form upon submission. _____

_____

_____

_____

_____

36. When were program outcomes measured? (select all that apply)
    ○ Baseline (before participants began the program)
    ○ During the program (How many times? ____)
    ○ Immediately after individuals completed the program
    ○ Subsequent Follow-up:
    ○ Once (___ months after the individuals completed the program)
    ○ Twice (second follow-up occurred ___ months after the individuals completed the program)
    ○ Three times (third follow-up occurred ___ months after the individuals completed the program)

Comparison Group

37. What comparison group was used for this evaluation?
    ◦ No comparison group was used
    ◦ Program participants were compared to themselves (looked at the difference between before they started the program and after completion)
        ◦ Convenience sample of similar individuals who, for example, were on the waiting list or engaging in usual care, but were *not* randomly assigned to those conditions. Describe: _____
        _____

        ◦ A group of similar individuals who were <u>randomly</u> assigned to a waitlist or to receive usual care. Please include detailed information on how the randomization process was designed and implemented. Describe: _____
        _____
        _____

        ◦ Other. Describe: _____
        _____

38. If there was a comparison group, how many people were included in the comparison group? _____ people.

39. If there was a comparison group, in what ways were the people in the comparison group the same or different from people in the evaluation? *(An example of a table is provided below. Revise and expand as necessary.)*

	People in the comparison group	People in the evaluation (program participants)	Are the two groups significantly different? ($p < 0.05$)
Female (%)			
Rank (in categories)			
Baseline measures (average and standard deviation; include all measures collected at any baseline assessment)			
Deployment in past 6 months (%)			

40. Use the table below to summarize the program evaluation.
    ◦ In the first row, list the type of data collected in each cycle. Examples include baseline (before the program began), program midpoint, immediately following program completion, or follow-up. Not all programs' evaluations will use all five columns. For example, a prepost design would record "baseline" above Time 1, "post-test" above Time 2, and would not use Time 3–5.
    ◦ In the second row, record the dates the data were collected.
    ◦ Program Outcome
        — Leave cells blank if they are not applicable to your evaluation.
        — All programs should fill in some data under primary outcome.

— If applicable to the program evaluation, data can be provided under secondary outcome and tertiary outcome, but this is not necessary.

— If the program outcome is measured as a percentage, list the percentage of people in the group who achieved the positive outcome (e.g., 25 percent report greater resilience). If the program outcome is measured on a scale, list the mean and standard deviation (e.g., *M = 17.6, SD = 3.6*).

— If the difference between the program participants and comparison group is statistically significant at the $p < 0.05$ level, place an asterisk (*) next to the percentage or mean.

Timing relative to the program cycle (e.g., baseline, first follow-up)

Dates of data collection

	Time 1 % or mean/ standard deviation	Time 2 % or mean/ standard deviation	Time 3 % or mean/ standard deviation	Time 4 % or mean/ standard deviation	Time 5 % or mean/ standard deviation
Primary outcome					
Program participants					
Comparison group					
Secondary outcome					
Program participants					
Comparison group					
Tertiary outcome					
Program participants					
Comparison group					

41. Describe any expected or unexpected negative/adverse effects experienced by program participants. _____
_____
_____
_____
_____

42. Name and contact information of outside evaluator (if applicable). _____
_____
_____
_____

Supporting materials may be attached. Please include:
- Program description materials
- Program manuals
- Scales or instruments used in any evaluation activities
- Published or unpublished evaluation findings

The RAND Program Expansion Tool and Instruction Manual

The RAND Program Expansion Tool (RPET) provides a standardized summary of the quality and outcome of a program evaluation. Please note that the RPET is designed to be used in conjunction with the RPET Instruction Manual, which follows the tool. Detailed scoring instructions for each item are listed in the instruction manual. The manual also includes justification for the scoring metrics and references for additional information on selected topics. New users will refer often to the manual for guidance; users with more experience may find the abbreviated instructions in italics sufficient to complete the tool.

Section I: Quality of the Evaluation

Evaluation Design

1. When did the program collect data or information about its outcomes? *[See Program Abstraction Form, question 36.]*

   0 At the beginning and end of the program, AND at least one appropriately timed follow-up after program completion

   1 At the beginning and end of the program

   1 At the end of the program only

   4 At the beginning of the program only

2. Were the outcomes of individuals in the program compared to another group as part of the evaluation? *[See Program Abstraction Form, question 37. Response (d) corresponds to a randomized control trial (RCT) and response (c) corresponds to a nonrandomized controlled trial. If the reviewer believes, based on the review of the entire evaluation, that the program incorrectly categorized the comparison group in their response on the Program Abstraction Form, the reviewer should override the program's categorization and respond based on the reviewer's understanding of the study design.]*

   0 Yes, and this was an RCT

   0 Yes, and this was a nonrandomized controlled trial

   1 Yes, but this was neither an RCT nor a controlled trial

   1 No, but this was a pre-post design

   4 No, they were not compared to other individuals

3. When determining program effectiveness, did the program evaluation use an intent-to-treat analysis (an analysis based on the original group assignment regardless of whether participants withdrew, dropped out, or pursued different treatment)? *[If an intent-to treat analysis is not used, see Program Abstraction Form, question 22, for the percentage who withdrew.]*

   0   Yes
   0   No, but fewer than 20 percent of participants withdrew from the program
   1   No, and 20–40 percent of participants withdrew from the program
   4   No, and more than 40 percent of participants withdrew from the program

Quality Rating for EVALUATION DESIGN:

   High   Moderate   Low

INSTRUCTIONS: Sum the results of questions 1–3.
   If sum = 0, circle high.
   If sum = 1–3, circle moderate.
   If sum = 4 or more, circle low.

Sample Used for the Evaluation

4. Was the response rate **at baseline (start of program or program evaluation)** adequate to prevent selection bias? *[See Program Abstraction Form, question 31a.]*

   0   Yes
   0   Not applicable—no baseline data collection
   1   No, but selection bias is unlikely to be severe
   5   No, and selection bias is likely to be significant

5. Was the response rate at **follow-up** adequate to prevent selection bias? *[See Program Abstraction Form, question 31b-e. Base judgment on highest value.]*

   0   Yes
   1   No, but selection bias is unlikely to be severe
   5   No, and selection bias is likely to be significant

6. To what extent were individuals who participated in the program evaluation representative of all individuals served by the program? *[See Program Abstraction Form, question 32.]*

   0   Very representative
   1   Somewhat representative
   5   Not representative
   5   Unknown, insufficient evidence

7. To what extent were the groups who participated in the evaluation (the group who received the program and the comparison group) similar? *[See Program Abstraction Form, question 39.]*

   0   The groups were similar on most or all characteristics
   0   This was a pre-post design (there was no comparison group)
   1   The groups were similar on many characteristics
   5   The groups were not similar

Quality Rating for SAMPLE:

   High   Moderate   Low

INSTRUCTIONS: Sum the results of questions 4–7.
> If sum = 0, circle high.
> If sum = 1–4, circle moderate.
> If sum = 5 or more, circle low.

Measurement

> *The following questions are for the first (primary) outcome.*

8. Was the outcome selected for evaluation relevant to the stated goals/purpose of the program? *[See Program Abstraction Form, questions 6, 33–35.]*
> 0   Yes, it was directly relevant
> 1   Somewhat. It was related, but not directly relevant
> 4   No, it was not relevant

9. What type(s) of data were collected? *[See Program Abstraction Form, questions 33–35.]*
> 0   An objectively measured outcome
> 0   Participant attitudes, symptoms, and/or functioning as reported or observed by someone other than the participant
> 0   Participant attitudes, symptoms, and/or functioning as reported by the participant on a validated self-report instrument
> 1   Participant attitudes, symptoms, and/or functioning as reported by the participant on a self-report instrument with unknown or poor psychometric properties
> 4   Participant satisfaction
> 4   Unknown, insufficient evidence

10. Was program success measured with a tool with good psychometric properties (e.g., reliability and validity)? *[See Program Abstraction Form, question 35.]*
> 0   Yes, the scale that was used to measure program outcome has good psychometric properties
> 0   Program outcome was not measured with a scale. It was measured using an objective, empirical outcome (e.g., number of doctor visits, employment status)
> 4   No, the scale that was used to measure program outcome has poor or unknown psychometric properties
> 4   Unknown, insufficient evidence

> *The following questions are for the second (secondary) outcome*

11. Was the secondary outcome selected for evaluation relevant to the stated goals/purpose of the program? *[Leave blank if no secondary outcome. Otherwise see Program Abstraction Form, questions 6, 33–35.]*
> 0   Yes, it was directly relevant
> 1   Somewhat. It was related, but not directly relevant
> 4   No, it was not relevant

12. What type of data was collected? *[Leave blank if no secondary outcome. Otherwise see Program Abstraction Form, questions 33–35.]*

   0   An objectively measured outcome

   0   Participant attitudes, symptoms, and/or functioning as reported or observed by someone other than the participant

   0   Participant attitudes, symptoms, and/or functioning as reported by the participant on a validated self-report instrument

   1   Participant attitudes, symptoms, and/or functioning as reported by the participant on a self-report instrument with unknown or poor psychometric properties

   4   Participant satisfaction

   4   Unknown, insufficient evidence

13. Was program success measured with a tool with good psychometric properties (e.g., reliability and validity)? *[Leave blank if no secondary outcome. Otherwise see Program Abstraction Form, question 35.]*

   0   Yes, the scale that was used to measure program outcome has good psychometric properties.

   0   Program outcome was not measured with a scale. It was measured using an objective, empirical outcome (e.g., number of doctor visits, employment status)

   4   No, the scale that was used to measure program outcome has poor or unknown psychometric properties.

   4   Unknown, insufficient evidence

Quality rating for PRIMARY OUTCOME:

   High   Moderate   Low

INSTRUCTIONS: Sum the results of questions 8–10.

   If sum = 0, circle high.
   If sum = 1–3, circle moderate.
   If sum = 4 or more, circle low.

Quality rating for SECONDARY OUTCOME:

   High   Moderate   Low   NA

INSTRUCTIONS: Circle NA, if no secondary outcome. Otherwise, sum the results of questions 11–13.

   If sum = 0, circle high.
   If sum = 1–3, circle moderate.
   If sum = 4 or more, circle low.

OVERALL QUALITY RATING
Rating for OVERALL QUALITY OF EVALUATION

   High   Moderate   Low

INSTRUCTIONS: Examine ratings for the evaluation design, sample used for the evaluation, and measurement. The following guidelines may be useful in assigning a rating for the overall quality.

- If all three components are rated "high," the overall quality should be rated "high."
- If not all components are rated "high," but no components are rated "low," the overall quality should be rated as "moderate."
- If any component is "low," the overall quality should be rated as "low."

In some circumstances, a reviewer may select a lower or higher quality rating than suggested based on his or her understanding of the program evaluation. See the instruction manual for guidance.

Section II: Program Effectiveness

14. Rate the effectiveness of the program on the primary and (if applicable) secondary outcome. *[See instruction manual for guidance.]* Note that the reviewer's estimate of effect size (from small to large) provides the opportunity to note the clinical significance of any statistically significant finding.

PRIMARY OUTCOME (circle)

Effective (moderate to large)   Effective (small)   Not Effective   Harmful

SECONDARY OUTCOME (circle if applicable)

Effective (moderate to large)   Effective (small)   Not Effective   Harmful

Notes for Program Effectiveness Rating: _____
_____
_____
_____
_____
_____
_____
_____
_____
_____
_____

Section III: Population Priority

15. Consider the population served by the program. Rate the extent to which the population is a current, exceptionally high-priority population to the DoD. Consider the extent to which the population served by the program is a sufficiently high priority such that it could conceivably change the expansion recommendation for the program. *[See instruction manual for guidance.]*

Is the POPULATION PRIORITY high?

Yes   No

Notes for Population Priority Rating: _____
_____
_____
_____
_____

Section IV: Policy Priority

16. Consider the political and social factors that will influence decisionmaking about the program and rate the extent to which political and social factors associated with the program are sufficiently strong that they could conceivably change the expansion recommendation for the program. *[See instruction manual for guidance.]*

Is the POLICY PRIORITY high?

Yes   No

Notes for Policy Priority Rating: _____
_____
_____
_____
_____

Section V: Summary Sheet

Figure B.1 summarizes the ratings for each of the four sections of the RPET. Starting at the left ("program information"), use each section's rating to select a branch. For example, at the first decision point, if the overall rating for the *quality of the evaluation* was "low," select the upper branch; if the overall rating for quality was "moderate" or "high," select the lower branch. Continue to the end of the tree and circle your recommendation. If your final recommendation does not match the one suggested by the decision tree, document your rationale (see Chapter Six).

Notes:_____
_____
_____
_____
_____

Figure B.1
Decision Tree

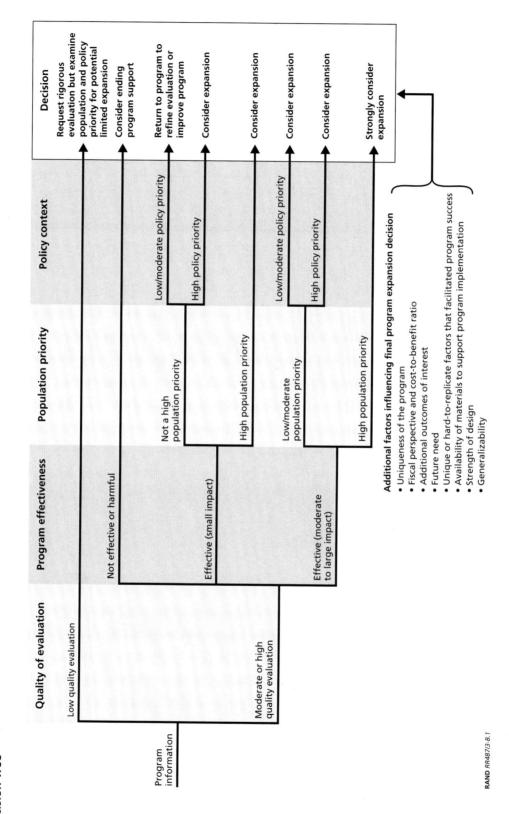

RAND *RR487/3-B.1*

Instruction Manual for the RAND Program Assessment Tool

Tool Description

The RAND Program Expansion Tool (RPET) is designed to be used by members of a decisionmaking body responsible for oversight of Department of Defense (DoD) programs for psychological health and traumatic brain injury (TBI). The RPET provides a mechanism by which program information can be summarized in a standard format to facilitate deliberations about program support or expansion. Although the RPET can help to organize information about the factors that should be considered during such deliberations, the decision itself remains in the hands of an appropriate oversight board or decisionmaker. That board or decisionmaker should also consider additional factors not captured by the RPET that may be unique to the circumstances of a particular program.

It is important to note that the RPET was designed to support the decisionmaking process and ensure that each program receives a fair and transparent review based on similar information. It is intended for use as a decisionmaking tool rather than as a quantifiable measure that provides a single score indicating the desirability of program expansion.

Suggested Users

Every attempt was made to make the RPET a flexible tool that is able to assist in the review of diverse programs that serve a variety of populations, use a range of interventions, and conduct dissimilar evaluations. Despite this effort, items appearing in the tool may not apply to all evaluations or to all programs. In these cases, the reviewers should use their best judgment to restructure the review process to meet the unique circumstances of an unusual program or evaluation strategy. Given this flexibility and reliance on reviewer expertise, it is recommended that tool users share certain characteristics.

The RPET is designed to be used by professionals with expertise in research and evaluation methodology and military health. The typical user will have at least master's-level training in evaluation or research methodology, be able to discriminate between designs for program evaluations (e.g., pre-post designs, controlled clinical trials, randomized controlled trials), have some exposure to statistics and hypothesis testing (e.g., p-values, effect sizes), and be able to identify common problems in evaluation design (e.g., small sample size, nonrepresentative samples). This instruction manual provides guidance to remind the user of key evaluation design considerations; however, this guidance should not be used in lieu of appropriate expertise.

Results from the RPET will then be shared with the decisionmaking board, which will have additional expertise in psychological health and TBI in a military context. Innovation in psychological health, military health care, and implementation of care in response to military operations proceeds at a tempo that cannot be matched by a static decision tool. Rather than building in current legal, social, and political priorities, the tool instead relies on the up-to-date expertise of the decisionmaking board to bring additional information about current operational needs, political realities, and social context. Thus, the board must have accurate knowledge of DoD infrastructure to support psychological health and the treatment of TBI, and be able to reflect on contemporary social and political pressures and priorities.

Item Responses

For each item, circle the number corresponding to the appropriate response for this evaluation.

The nontraditional response scaling (0, 1, or 4/5) is algebraically designed to simplify the overall scoring for each section. Any item response that corresponds to a "by-the-book" program evaluation is assigned a "0" (highest quality), any nonideal strategy that nonetheless provides useful data is assigned a "1" (moderate quality), and any fatal flaw in the evaluation design is assigned a large number—a "4" or "5" (low quality). This backward scaling ensures that when all responses are added, only evaluations that completed the entire domain "by the book" receive a "high" quality score and any evaluation with one or more fatal flaws automatically receives a "low" quality score for the domain.

Though this rubric will work for scoring the vast majority of programs, there may be unique programs or situations that warrant a slightly different score. In these cases, the user should score as they see fit, making note of the context and providing a justification for the score for further consideration of the decisionmaking board.

Item-by-Item Instructions

Section I: Quality of the Evaluation

Section I rates the quality of the program evaluation. There are three components to this section.

Evaluation Design

Questions in this section assess the overall strength of the design of the program evaluation. This section includes an assessment of the *comparison group* (see text box for definition).

Comparison Group

A group of people who did not participate in the program (McDavid and Hawthorn, 2006). The performance of people in the comparison group relative to the performance of people who were served by the program helps decisionmakers understand if the program helped people, hurt people, or did not affect them.

Definitions

Sample: A relatively small number of individuals drawn from a population for inclusion in a study (Bordens and Abbott, 1996). For program evaluations, the sample is all of the individuals who were included in the evaluation.

Representative sample: A sample of participants in which the characteristics of all program participants are adequately represented (Bordens and Abbot, 1996). For program evaluations, a sample is representative if the people who participated in the evaluation were similar to the people who are served by the program but did not participate in the evaluation.

Sample Used for the Evaluation

Questions assessing the sample are designed to determine whether the program evaluation used a *representative sample* (see text box for definition).

Collecting information from a representative sample is important for ensuring that the evaluation results accurately depict the results of the program overall. For example, if a program based the evaluation only on those people who completed the program and a large proportion of people dropped out prior to program completion, the program may appear more successful than it really is. To ensure a representative sample, it would be important to include every type of person served by the program.

Measurement

Questions assessing the measurement strategy are designed to ensure that the program evaluation measured an appropriate outcome that matched the goals of the program and that the measurement strategy was sound.

Evaluation Design: Instructions
ITEM 1. When did the program collect data or information about its outcomes?
0 At the beginning and end of the program, AND at least one appropriately timed follow-up after program completion
1 At the beginning and end of the program
1 At the end of the program only
4 At the beginning of the program only

INSTRUCTIONS (Item 1)
Program responses can be used to inform this item. See Program Abstraction Form, question 36. For the first question, the reviewer is tasked with determining whether a follow-up assessment was appropriately timed. Timing should be adequate to ensure that participants have had the opportunity to encounter the situations or stressors that the program was designed to help (e.g., postdeployment for a resilience training program). Note that for some programs, the end of the program may also be an appropriate follow-up time point; the reviewer should circle the first response in this case.

BACKGROUND (Item 1)

Typically, the longer the time horizon after program completion that outcomes are measured, the stronger the test of efficacy. When outcomes are measured immediately after program completion, success may be overstated. For example, service members who have just completed a resiliency training program may feel confident in their ability to use resilience skills and/or may be motivated to report confidence out of gratitude or respect for program leaders. However, if these same service members were contacted three months later, they might more realistically report that the skills were difficult to implement or proved to be only marginally helpful. For this reason, evaluations with longer follow-up periods are considered to be stronger tests of program efficacy (McDavid and Hawthorn, 2006).

SCORING JUSTIFICATION (Item 1)

Evaluations that measure outcomes at an appropriate follow-up time point in addition to baseline measurement receive the strongest rating (0). Programs that measure outcomes immediately following the program but do not include a follow-up may still identify improvement (or lack thereof) among program participants, and therefore, receive a "moderate" rating (1). Evaluations that report no outcomes following program participation are inadequate to assess program performance and therefore receive a "low" rating (4).

ITEM 2. Were the outcomes of individuals in the program compared to another group as part of the evaluation?

    0   Yes, and this was a randomized controlled trial (RCT)

    0   Yes, and this was a nonrandomized controlled trial

    1   Yes, but this was neither an RCT nor a controlled trial

    1   No, but this was a pre-post design

    4   No, they were not compared to other individuals

INSTRUCTIONS (Item 2)

Program responses (Table C.1) can be used to inform Item #2. See Program Abstraction Form, question 37, for the program's description of the comparison group. Response (d) from Q. 37 corresponds to an RCT, and response (c) corresponds to a nonrandomized controlled trial (see Background section for a description of these terms). If the reviewer believes, based on the review of the entire evaluation, that the program incorrectly categorized the comparison group in their response on the Program Abstraction Form, the reviewer should override the program's categorization and respond based on the reviewer's understanding of the evaluation design.

BACKGROUND (Item 2)

Mental health and TBI symptoms can change over time for many reasons. Some illnesses come and go (e.g., depression), others may naturally remit (e.g., acute stress disorder), and some may not appear until several months after exposure to an event. Sometimes people find help for their problems in settings like religious or community organizations. Others may find their own solutions (e.g., exercise, journaling) or receive care in another setting. Skills learned in programs may degrade over time if not used in a timely way. Program evaluations should be designed in a way that helps the decisionmaker understand whether observed improvement among participants was due to the program's activities or due to another factor.

A good program evaluation provides compelling evidence that program participants improved on an outcome of interest AND that the program was responsible for that improve-

Table C.1
Program Responses for Item 2

Response	Description	Example
0—Yes, and this was a randomized controlled trial (RCT).	Prior to beginning the evaluation, potential program participants were randomly assigned to participate in the program or not to participate. The people who are not assigned to receive the intervention may be placed on a waiting list, receive no intervention, or receive typical care. The outcomes of people who were randomly assigned to participate were compared to the outcomes of people who were randomly assigned not to participate.	After completing a deployment, half of the members of the division are assigned at random to complete a new psychological health program. The remaining service members attend a typical postdeployment debriefing session only. Six months later, the psychological health of service members who were randomly selected to attend the program is compared to the psychological health of service members who were not selected to attend the program.
0—Yes, and this was a nonrandomized controlled trial.	Program participants were compared to a group of similar individuals. Although assignment is not random, the investigators use strategies to ensure that the groups are similar. The people who are not assigned to receive the intervention may be placed on a waiting list, receive no intervention, or receive typical care.	A division returning from a deployment participates in a new psychological health program. Six months later, their health is compared to the health of service members who returned to a different base that did not have the psychological health program.
1—Yes, but this was neither an RCT nor a controlled trial.	Program participants were compared to another group of individuals, but they were not randomly assigned and/or the extent to which they were similar to the group who received the program is not clear.	An infantry battalion returning from a deployment participates in a new psychological health program and is compared to a logistics support battalion also returning from deployment. The reviewer suspects that the two groups not only have different responsibilities, but also were exposed to different conditions during deployment.
1—No, but this was a pre-post design.	Participants' scores after program completion were compared to their own scores before they began the program.	A military group returning from a deployment participates in a new psychological health program. Each person's score at the start of the program is compared with his or her score six months later to determine if psychological health declined or improved over time.
4—No.	There is no comparison group and participants' scores are measured only once.	A military group returning from a deployment participates in a new psychological health program. Their psychological health is measured one time only. The reviewer cannot tell if this score is better, the same, or worse than it would be without the program.

ment. The best way to do this is to compare program participants to people who are very similar to the participants but who did not receive program services (Basham, 1986). People in both groups should experience the same benefit of time, community resources, and self-help, and should ideally be exposed to similar conditions (e.g., similar deployment experiences). If both groups are similar and people in the program do better than the comparison group, then decisionmakers generally can be confident that the improvement can be ascribed to the program.

A randomized controlled trial (RCT) is an ideal evaluation design (Hartman et al., 2002; Oakes and Kaufman, 2006). A group of people who are eligible to participate in the program are divided randomly. Some are assigned to receive program services and some are assigned not to receive the program services (the comparison group). After the program is over, the two groups are compared to see if the program participants are functioning better than the nonparticipants. RCTs are very strong designs, because the two groups should be similar on a variety of domains, and therefore it is reasonable to ascribe any difference between the groups to the treatment. Unfortunately, in many cases it is not possible or appropriate to randomly assign people to participate in a program or to be part of a control group.

A nonrandomized controlled trial is a design that includes a comparison group who did not receive the program services, but were not randomly assigned (Basham, 1986). Possible comparison groups include people who are still waiting to participate in the program, people who are participating in a different program, or people who have the same condition but are not in the program. This design provides useful data to determine the effectiveness of the program. However, caution must be used in interpretation. The two groups may differ in ways that are unrelated to treatment. The comparison group may be healthier or more impaired than program participants and this will complicate interpretation of the results.

In a pre-post design, participants are compared to themselves. Before beginning the program, measures of participant performance are collected. After completing the program, the same measures are collected again. Each participant's performance after the program is compared to his or her own performance before the program to determine whether he or she improved, worsened, or remained the same. This is a popular and useful design, but again, caution should be used in interpreting the results. Sometimes performance improves over time regardless of program participation, and it can be difficult to determine if improvement is due to the program or some other factor. Similarly, sometimes performance can worsen over time, and this can cause a program to appear unhelpful (e.g., no difference between pre- and post-program functioning) when it may actually have prevented participants from getting worse.

JUSTIFICATION (Item 2)

Randomized controlled trials and nonrandomized controlled trials are assigned the highest quality rating (0) because these designs all produce data that will allow decisionmakers to draw conclusions (although with caveats in some cases) about the effectiveness of the program. Given the difficulty in conducting a gold standard assessment (RCT) in settings with limited resources, we deemed it unrealistic to limit the "high" quality rating to this design only. Designs with comparison groups that may not be well-matched to the treatment group and pre-post designs are assigned quality ratings of "moderate" (1) as it will be difficult to determine whether outcomes should be attributed to the program or differences between the groups. Program evaluations without comparison groups or baseline assessments are impossible to interpret and therefore receive a "low" quality rating (4).

ITEM 3. When determining program effectiveness, did the program evaluation use an intent-to-treat analysis?

    0 Yes

    0 No, but fewer than 20 percent of participants withdrew from the program

    1 No, and 20–40 percent of participants withdrew from the program

    4 No, and more than 40 percent of participants withdrew from the program

INSTRUCTIONS (Item 3)

See definition of intent-to-treat analysis in the box and compare the definition with the information provided by the program to determine whether an intent-to-treat analysis was used.

> ### Intent-to-Treat Analysis
>
> An analysis based on the outcomes of everyone who was assigned to participate in a program regardless of whether they completed the program, withdrew, dropped out, or pursued a different option (Fisher et al.,1990).

If an intent-to-treat analysis was not used, clarify the extent to which this affects the methodological quality by specifying the percentage of participants who withdrew from the program prior to completion. See Program Abstraction Form, question 22, for this information.

BACKGROUND (Item 3)

When a program experiences significant dropout and intent-to-treat analyses are not employed, the results of a program evaluation can be biased, skewed, or incorrect (Fisher et al., 1990). If people who have more significant problems drop out more frequently than people who have mild problems, even an ineffective program may appear to be helpful. Intent-to-treat analyses may not be necessary when the dropout rate is low.

JUSTIFICATION (Item 3)

There is no gold standard to dictate the precise value of the allowable dropout rate. For the RPET, we have set a lenient rate of up to 20 percent that can still receive a "high" quality rating (0). Although the RPET recommends 20–40 percent as the rate at which an intent-to-treat analysis would be preferable (1), decisionmakers may still wish to interpret evaluation results provided they acknowledge the caveat of the potential bias introduced by a high dropout rate. A rate over 40 percent without an intent-to-treat analysis represents a fatal flaw in the evaluation design and receives a "low" quality rating (4). Given the lack of scholarly consensus about precise cutoffs, the reviewer should exercise his or her own discretion on this item when necessary.

Quality rating for EVALUATION DESIGN:

High   Moderate   Low

INSTRUCTIONS: Sum the results of questions 1–3

  If sum = 0, circle high.
  If sum = 1–3, circle moderate.
  If sum = 4 or more, circle low.

JUSTIFICATION (Item 3)

A "high" quality rating is assigned if the program evaluation was conducted "by the book"—that is, the evaluation design was strong, outcomes were measured at appropriate time points, and intent-to-treat analyses were used when appropriate (Bordens and Abbott, 1996; Cohen and Swerdlik, 2002; McDavid and Hawthorn, 2006).

A "moderate" rating is assigned if the evaluation design was not ideal according to standard recommendations for "high" quality program evaluations (Bordens and Abbott, 1996; Cohen and Swerdlik, 2002; McDavid and Hawthorn, 2006). However, the data may still be of relevance to a decisionmaker or decisionmaking body, provided they are aware of possible problems with the data and can take those problems into account when making their decision.

A "low" quality rating is assigned if there was a fatal flaw in the evaluation design (Bordens and Abbott, 1996; Cohen and Swerdlik, 2002; McDavid and Hawthorn, 2006). The flaw is of such significance that the results of the program evaluation should not be used to make inferences about program success.

Sample Used for the Evaluation: Instructions

ITEM 4. Was the response rate at baseline (start of program or program evaluation) adequate to prevent selection bias?

  0 Yes
  0 Not applicable—no baseline data collection
  1 No, but selection bias is unlikely to be severe
  5 No, and selection bias is likely to be significant

INSTRUCTIONS (Item 4)

Use the percentage provided by program to guide response. See the Program Abstraction Form, question 31a.

BACKGROUND (Item 4)

Selection bias can occur when *response rates* are low (see text box for definitions).

People may agree or decline to participate in an evaluation for a variety of reasons. Common reasons for declining to take part in an evaluation include lack of time, indifferent or negative feelings toward the program, or not attending the program when data are collected. If a large percentage of people are left out of an evaluation, the evaluation may produce misleading results. For example, imagine that people are asked to stay after a session to fill out evaluation paperwork and only 50 percent of the people agree to do so. Those who stay behind are probably different from the people who left; they may be less busy or have stronger feelings about program. Alternatively, if the people most adversely affected by a condition drop out of the program, and therefore are not included in the evaluation, selection bias would also be present.

JUSTIFICATION (Item 4)

"High" quality ratings (0) are assigned to programs for which selection bias during the baseline assessment has been ruled out (either because the response rate is high or because baseline data collection was unnecessary). A "moderate" rating (1) is assigned when there is evidence of selection bias, but the reviewer determines that will not invalidate program outcome conclusions. A "low" quality rating is assigned (5) when the reviewer determines that the selection bias at baseline invalidates all program outcome conclusions.

Definitions

Response Rate: The number of people who participate in an evaluation divided by the number of people who were invited to participate.

Selection Bias: Deviation between the characteristics of people who participated in the evaluation and those who did not (Bordens and Abbott, 1996).

ITEM 5. Was the response rate at follow-up adequate to prevent selection bias?

0 Yes
1 No, but selection bias is unlikely to be severe
5 No, and selection bias is likely to be significant

INSTRUCTIONS (Item 5)

Use the percentage provided by program to guide response. See the Program Abstraction Form, question 31b-e. If program conducted multiple waves of follow-up, base the judgment on the highest value.

BACKGROUND (Item 5)

See Item 4 above.

JUSTIFICATION (Item 5)

See Item 4 above.

ITEM 6. To what extent were individuals who participated in the program evaluation representative of all individuals who were served by the program?

0 Very representative
1 Somewhat representative
5 Not representative
5 Unknown, insufficient evidence

INSTRUCTIONS (Item 6)

See Program Abstraction Form, question 32, for a comparison of sample demographics of people in the evaluation relative to all program participants. Reviewers may also wish to consider other factors that could affect sample representativeness and should rely on their own expertise to make this judgment. Use the descriptions below to select a response.

BACKGROUND (Item 6)

If the people who participate in an evaluation differ in key ways from other people who use the program, then information about program outcomes may not be generalizable (Bordens

Table C.2
Program Responses for Item 6

Response	Description
0—Very representative	The reviewer believes that the characteristics of the evaluation sample matched the characteristics of all program participants.
1—Somewhat representative	The reviewer notes that some characteristics of the evaluation sample differ from the characteristics of the program participants. However, the reviewer believes that the evaluation results are still relevant and should be considered, provided decisionmakers are aware of possible problems with the sample.
5—Not representative	The reviewer believes that the evaluation sample is fundamentally different than program participants on important characteristics. Given these important differences, the results reported in the evaluation cannot be generalized to other program participants.
5—Unknown, insufficient evidence	The program evaluation does not include the information necessary to make this judgment.
4—No.	There is no comparison group and participants' scores are measured only once.

and Abbott, 1996; McDavid and Hawthorn, 2006). Imagine that a marriage enhancement program collected outcome data only from couples who had been married 10 or more years (i.e., a nonrepresentative sample). They may incorrectly conclude that the program prevented divorce. Instead, they collect data from couples whose relationship has already withstood the test of time and failed to collect similar data from younger or newly married couples who may be at a higher risk for divorce. Representativeness of the sample is considered a key criterion by which to judge program evaluation quality (McDavid and Hawthorn, 2006).

JUSTIFICATION (Item 6)

A "high" quality rating (0) is assigned to programs with representative samples. A "moderate" rating (1) is assigned when there is evidence that the sample is not fully representative, but not to the extent that it will invalidate program outcome conclusions. A "low" quality rating (5) is assigned when the reviewer determines that the sample is not representative and program outcome conclusions are therefore invalid or when the information necessary to make this determination is unavailable.

ITEM 7. To what extent were the groups who participated in the evaluation (the group who received the program and the comparison group) similar?

    0   The groups were similar on most or all characteristics
    0   This was a pre-post design (there was no comparison group)
    1   The groups were similar on many characteristics
    5   The groups were not similar

INSTRUCTIONS (Item 7)

Program responses can be used to inform this item. See Program Abstraction Form, question 39, for a description of the comparison group (if used) and a table that describes any group differences between the treatment and comparison group.

BACKGROUND (Item 7)

Ideally, the treatment and comparison group are similar on all characteristics with the exception of program participation. When this is the case, any improvement observed among program participants can be attributed to the program. Interpretation of evaluation results is significantly more complicated when the treatment and comparison groups differ from one another in many ways. For example, if service members who receive resiliency training are less likely to be deployed than the comparison group, and subsequently appeared more resilient to stress when using standard measures, the evaluator should consider whether this positive outcome is due to reduced combat exposure rather than to the effects of the program itself.

JUSTIFICATION (Item 7)

A "high" quality rating (0) is assigned when the comparison and treatment group are well-matched or when participants are effectively compared to themselves (a pre-post design). A "moderate" rating (1) is assigned when the treatment and comparison group are not perfectly matched, but the reviewer believes any discrepancy is limited and will not invalidate the program outcome conclusions. A "low" quality rating (5) is assigned when the reviewer determines that the treatment and comparison group are not similar, and therefore any outcome differences between the groups cannot be definitely assigned to the effect of the program.

Quality Rating for SAMPLE

High   Moderate   Low

INSTRUCTIONS: Sum the results of questions 4–7.
>   If sum = 0, circle high.
>   If sum = 1–4, circle moderate.
>   If sum = 5 or more, circle low.

JUSTIFICATION

A "high" quality rating is assigned if the program evaluation was conducted "by the book;" that is, if all important sample characteristics were addressed according to recommendations for high-quality program evaluation (McDavid and Hawthorn, 2006).

A "moderate" quality rating is assigned if the program evaluation was not ideal according to standard recommendations for high-quality program evaluations (McDavid and Hawthorn, 2006). However, the data may still be of relevance to a decisionmaker or decisionmaking body, provided they are aware of possible problems with the data and can take those problems into account when making their decision.

A "low" quality rating is assigned if the program evaluation has a fatal flaw (McDavid and Hawthorn, 2006) as measured by any item. The flaw is of such significance that the results of the program evaluation should not be used to make inferences about program success.

Measurement: Instructions

ITEM 8. Was the outcome selected for evaluation relevant to the stated goals/purpose of the program?
>   0 Yes, it was directly relevant
>   1 Somewhat. It was related, but not directly relevant
>   4 No, it was not relevant

INSTRUCTIONS (Item 8)

Program responses can be used to inform this item. See Program Abstraction Form, question 6, for program mission and goals and questions 33–35 for measurement strategy.

A common mistake in conducting program evaluations is to measure an outcome that is not closely related to the goal of the program. For example, if a program's goal is to improve resilience to psychological stressors, participant satisfaction (how much people liked the program) would not be an appropriate outcome. A stronger evaluation would include measures of how well participants coped with psychological stressors during their deployment. Use the descriptions below to select a response.

BACKGROUND (Item 8)

In order to know if a program is meeting its self-defined goal, the measured outcome must be related to the goal (McDavid and Hawthorn, 2006).

JUSTIFICATION (Item 8)

A "high" quality rating (0) is assigned when the measured outcome directly matches the program's goal. A "moderate" quality rating (1) is assigned when the measured outcome is a proxy or indirectly related to the program's goal. A "low" quality rating (4) is assigned when the measured outcome is unrelated to the stated goals of the program.

Table C.3
Program Responses for Item 8

Response	Description	Example
0—Yes, it was directly relevant.	The outcome measured matches at least one of the program's goals or its mission.	A program seeks to improve resilience during a deployment and measures the percentage of service members who experience mental health problems following deployment.
1—Somewhat. It was related, but not directly relevant.	The outcome is linked to the programs goals, but it does not match exactly. This often occurs when the outcome occurs infrequently or when measurement of the outcome is very difficult or sensitive.	A program is designed to reduce domestic violence within the military community. Given difficulty obtaining accurate estimates of families in which domestic violence occurs, the program measures participant responses to the question "How likely would you be to step in, say something, or intervene if you thought domestic violence was occurring in one of your colleague's families?"
4—No, it was not relevant.	The outcome is not linked to the program's goals or mission.	A program seeks to reduce posttraumatic stress disorder (PTSD) among returning service members, but instead of tracking PTSD diagnoses, measures participants' satisfaction (how much people liked or enjoyed the program).
1—No, but this was a pre-post design.	Participants' scores after program completion were compared to their own scores before they began the program.	A military group returning from a deployment participates in a new psychological health program. Each person's score at the start of the program is compared with his or her score six months later to determine if psychological health declined or improved over time.
4—No.	There is no comparison group and participants' scores are measured only once.	A military group returning from a deployment participates in a new psychological health program. Their psychological health is measured one time only. The reviewer cannot tell if this score is better, the same, or worse than it would be without the program.

ITEM 9. What type(s) of data were collected?

0   An objectively measured outcome

0   Participant attitudes, symptoms, and/or functioning as reported or observed by someone other than the participant

0   Participant attitudes, symptoms, and/or functioning as reported by the participant on a validated self-report instrument

1   Participant attitudes, symptoms, and/or functioning as reported by the participant on a self-report instrument with unknown or poor psychometric properties

4   Participant satisfaction

4   Unknown, insufficient evidence

INSTRUCTIONS (Item 9)

Program responses can be used to inform this item. See Program Abstraction Form, questions 33–35, for a description of the measurement strategy. Use the descriptions below to select a response. If more than one type of data was collected, select the strongest outcome that was measured (i.e., response option with the lowest numeric value).

Programs are instructed to provide documentation to support the psychometrics of any measurement strategy, particularly for self-reported scales. If such documentation is not included, the reviewer can consult the RAND Online Repository of Measures for Evaluating

Table C.4
Program Responses for Item 9

Response	Description	Example
0—An objectively measured outcome	A readily observable outcome that does not rely on the participant or program's judgment or perception	Number of psychiatric hospitalizations, divorce rates
0—Participant attitudes, symptoms, and/or functioning as reported or observed by someone other than the participant	Scales, questionnaires, diagnoses (completed by someone other than the participant)	Commander reports of service member performance, psychiatrist diagnoses before and after the program, employer's reports of job functioning
0—Participant attitudes, symptoms, and/or functioning as reported by the participant on a validated self-report instrument	Scales, questionnaires, interviews with strong psychometric properties completed by the participant	Beck Depression Inventory score, Hamilton Anxiety Scale score
1—Participant attitudes, symptoms, and/or functioning as reported by the participant on a self-report instrument with unknown or poor psychometric properties	Scales, questionnaires, interviews completed by the participant with poor psychometrics or that have never been evaluated	A questionnaire to assess stress during deployment is developed by the program, but scale reliability and validity has not been assessed.
4—Participant satisfaction	Scales assessing the extent to which participants liked or enjoyed the program	Respondents rate the degree to which they "enjoyed the program" and "believe it helped them."
4—Unknown, insufficient evidence	Select this response when evaluation does not include enough information to allow reviewer to classify the type of outcome.	Evaluation indicates that the outcome was "depression" without specifying if depression was defined by a psychiatric hospitalization, a suicide attempt, psychiatrist or physician diagnosis, or participant report of symptoms, or measures outcomes that are not linked to program goals.

Psychological Health and Traumatic Brain Injury Programs for detailed information about scale psychometrics (Acosta, Reynolds, et al., 2014).

BACKGROUND (Item 9)

Objectively measured outcomes are less vulnerable to measurement bias than other measurement strategies; as such, they provided the strongest evidence in favor a program (Bordens and Abbott, 1996; Cohen and Swerdlik, 2002; McDavid and Hawthorn, 2006). Self-reported data are vulnerable to a variety of biases but nonetheless can provide important information about program outcome, particularly when assessed using well-validated scales (Cohen and Swerdlik, 2002). When outcomes are reported by someone other than the participants, biases are often minimized (Cohen and Swerdlik, 2002).

JUSTIFICATION (Item 9)

A "high" quality rating (0) is assigned when the outcome is measured in a way that maximizes validity, including objective or empirical outcomes, reports from an observer, or self-reports on a validated scale. Although these three strategies can be argued to differ in their validity, all produce data that should be strongly linked with the outcome of interest. A "moderate" quality rating (1) is assigned when the outcome is measured with an instrument that has not been validated, and therefore the reviewer is uncertain of the strength of the association with the outcome of interest. The reviewer should use his or her judgment and assign this rating only if he or she believes that the outcome measure could reasonably be expected to be associated with the outcome. A "low" quality rating (4) is assigned when participant satisfaction is the only outcome measure. Participants may "like" a program that does not help them in the long run, and therefore, satisfaction is not necessarily related to the effectiveness of the program. A "low" rating may also be assigned if the reviewer has insufficient information to assess the quality of the outcome measure.

ITEM 10. Was program success measured with a tool with good psychometric properties (e.g., reliability and validity)?

    0 Yes, the scale that was used to measure program outcome has good psychometric properties

    0 Program outcome was not measured with a scale. It was measured using an objective, empirical outcome (e.g., number of doctor visits, employment status)

    4 No, the scale that was used to measure program outcome has poor or unknown psychometric properties.

    4 Unknown, insufficient evidence

INSTRUCTIONS (Item 10)

Program responses can be used to inform this item. See Program Abstraction Form, question 35. Use the descriptions below to select a response.

- If more than one scale was used, circle the strongest response that applies (e.g., response with the lowest numeric value)
- Participant satisfaction (how much they "liked" or enjoyed the program) is generally not a relevant outcome. Reviewers should circle "unknown, insufficient evidence" if program satisfaction is the only outcome provide by the program

BACKGROUND (Item 10)

If important policy and funding decisions will be made based on data collected using a scale or questionnaire, that scale or questionnaire should be a strong and defensible measurement strategy. A strong program evaluation will measure outcomes using a questionnaire or survey that is reliable and valid (Cohen and Swerdlik, 2002; McDavid and Hawthorn, 2006). Most program evaluations will rely on scales and questionnaires to assess psychological outcomes; however, program success can be measured in some cases using an objective outcome. When this is the case, psychometric data may not necessary.

Definitions

Reliability: The extent to which measurements are consistent or repeatable (Cohen and Swerdlik, 2002).

Validity: The extent to which a scale or questionnaire measures the outcome it claims to measure (Cohen and Swerdlik, 2002).

Table C.5
Program Responses for Item 10

Response	Description	Example
0—Yes, the scale that was used to measure program outcome has good psychometric properties.	The program selected a measurement scale that has been shown to be reliable and valid and included information to support this claim.	Depression was measured with the Beck Depression Inventory (which has strong documented psychometrics). Coping during deployment was measured with a questionnaire designed by the program; the program conducted their own psychometric analysis of the new scale and provided data to support the scale's reliability and validity.
0—Program outcome was not measured with a scale. It was measured using an objective, empirical outcome.	Some outcomes are objective, and therefore, do not require information about psychometrics. Use this response if the outcome is measured directly and requires no inference or judgment by the program or person providing the information.	Number of psychiatric hospitalizations; divorce rates
4—No, the scale that was used to measure program outcome has poor or unknown psychometric properties.	The program selected a scale that does not meet standard criteria for reliability and validity OR a scale that has not been evaluated for reliability of validity.	Depression was measured with a one-item assessment of depression. Coping during deployment was measured with a questionnaire designed by the program; the program cannot provide information about the scale's psychometrics.
4—Unknown, insufficient evidence	Use when evaluation does not include enough information to allow reviewer to classify the type of outcome.	Program claims psychometrics are strong, but does not supply supporting material.

JUSTIFICATION (Item 10)

A "high" quality rating (0) is assigned when the outcome measure is reliable and valid *OR* when an objective outcome measure is used. These requirements ensure that the collected data is associated with the real outcome of interest. A "low" quality rating (4) is assigned if psychometrics are poor or unknown. When psychometrics are poor, the reviewer cannot be certain if the measured outcomes accurately reflect the true outcome of interest, and therefore, the program evaluation cannot be used to draw conclusions about the success of the program.

ITEM 11. Was the secondary outcome selected for evaluation relevant to the stated goals/purpose of the program?

    0 Yes, it was directly relevant
    1 Somewhat. It was related, but not directly relevant
    4 No, it was not relevant

INSTRUCTIONS (Item 11)

Leave blank if the program has no secondary outcome. Otherwise, see Item 8 for instructions.

BACKGROUND (Item 11)

See Item 8 for background.

JUSTIFICATION (Item 11)

See Item 8 for justification.

ITEM 12. What type of data was collected?

0   An objectively measured outcome

0   Participant attitudes, symptoms, and/or functioning as reported or observed by some-one other than the participant

0   Participant attitudes, symptoms, and/or functioning as reported by the participant on a validated self-report instrument

1   Participant attitudes, symptoms, and/or functioning as reported by the participant on a self-report instrument with unknown or poor psychometric properties

4   Participant satisfaction

4   Unknown, insufficient evidence

INSTRUCTIONS (Item 12)
Leave blank if the program has no secondary outcome. Otherwise, see Item 9 for instructions.

BACKGROUND (Item 12)
See Item 9 for background.

JUSTIFICATION (Item 12)
See Item 9 for justification.

ITEM 13. Was program success measured with a tool with good psychometric properties (e.g., reliability and validity)?

0   Yes, the scale that was used to measure program outcome has good psychometric properties.

0   Program outcome was not measured with a scale. It was measured using an objective, empirical outcome (e.g., number of doctor visits, employment status).

4   No, the scale that was used to measure program outcome has poor or unknown psychometric properties.

4   Unknown, insufficient evidence

INSTRUCTIONS (Item 13)
Leave blank if the program has no secondary outcome. Otherwise, see Item 10 for instructions.

BACKGROUND (Item 13)
See Item 10 for background.

JUSTIFICATION (Item 13)
See Item 10 for justification.

MEASUREMENT

Quality rating for PRIMARY OUTCOME:

High	Moderate	Low	

Quality rating for SECONDARY OUTCOME:

High	Moderate	Low	NA

INSTRUCTIONS

For Primary Outcome, sum the results of questions 8–10

    If sum = 0, circle high.

    If sum = 1-3, circle moderate.

    If sum = 4 or more, circle low.

For Secondary Outcome, sum the results of questions 11–13

    If no secondary outcome, circle NA.

    If sum = 0, circle high.

    If sum = 1-3, circle moderate.

    If sum = 4 or more, circle low.

JUSTIFICATION

A "high" quality rating is assigned if the program evaluation was conducted "by the book," that is, the evaluation measured an outcome that matched the program's goals, the measurement was objective or completed by an observer (rather than the participant), and the measurement strategy was psychometrically sound (Bordens and Abbott, 1996; Cohen and Swerdlik, 2002; McDavid and Hawthorn, 2006).

A "moderate" quality rating is assigned if the program evaluation was not ideal according to standard recommendations for high-quality program evaluations (Bordens and Abbott, 1996; Cohen and Swerdlik, 2002; McDavid and Hawthorn, 2006). However, the data may still be of relevance to a decisionmaker or decisionmaking body, provided they are aware of possible problems with the data and can take those problems into account when making their decision.

A "low" quality rating is assigned if there was a fatal flaw in the measurement of the program outcome (Bordens and Abbott, 1996; Cohen and Swerdlik, 2002; McDavid and Hawthorn, 2006). The flaw is of such significance that the results of the program evaluation should not be used to make inferences about program success.

OVERALL QUALITY RATING

Based on your assessment of the quality of the evaluation design, sample used for the evaluation, and measurement above, what is your overall rating for the quality of the evaluation?

Rating for OVERALL QUALITY OF THE EVALUATION

    High   Moderate   Low

INSTRUCTIONS

Examine ratings for the evaluation design, sample used for the evaluation, and measurement. The following guidelines may be useful in assigning a rating for the overall quality.

- If all three components are rated as "high," rate overall quality as "high."
- If not all components are "high," but no components are "low," rate overall quality "moderate."
- If any component is "low," rate the overall quality "low."

The instructions above for determining overall quality are guidelines, and the reviewer should rely on his or her own expertise to make a final judgment about the quality of the evaluation. He or she may choose to select a lower or higher quality rating than suggested above based on his or her understanding of the program evaluation. Given that this tool was designed to be used by a variety of programs implementing a wide variety of program evaluation strategies, it is impossible to account for all possible design challenges or to imagine all the approaches that will be used by creative evaluation designers. In some cases, the format of this evaluation tool may not fit neatly with a novel evaluation design, and the reviewer should be free to use his or her judgment to provide a rating that more closely matches the true strength (or weakness) of an evaluation.

Please note: If the reviewer chooses to assign a rating that is inconsistent with the suggested rating strategy above, please document the rationale.

JUSTIFICATION

A "high" quality rating is suggested if the program evaluation was conducted "by the book," for all domains (Bordens and Abbott, 1996; Cohen and Swerdlik, 2002; McDavid and Hawthorn, 2006).

A "moderate" quality rating is suggested if the evaluation design was not ideal according to standard recommendations for high-quality program evaluations (Bordens and Abbott, 1996; Cohen and Swerdlik, 2002; McDavid and Hawthorn, 2006). However, the data may still be of relevance to a decisionmaker or decisionmaking body provided they are aware of possible problems with the data and can take those problems into account when making their decision.

A "low" quality rating is suggested if there was a fatal flaw on any domain (Bordens and Abbott, 1996; Cohen and Swerdlik, 2002; McDavid and Hawthorn, 2006). The flaw is of such significance that the results of the program evaluation should not be used to make inferences about program success.

Section II: Program Effectiveness
ITEM 14. Rate the effectiveness of the program on the primary and (if applicable) secondary outcome.

PRIMARY OUTCOME (circle)

Effective (moderate to large)   Effective (small)   Not Effective   Harmful

SECONDARY OUTCOME (circle if applicable)

Effective (moderate to large)   Effective (small)   Not Effective   Harmful

INSTRUCTIONS (Item 14)
Program responses can be used to inform this item. The reviewer should compare the data provided in the Program Abstraction Form, question 40, to the categories described below. This question prompts the reviewer to estimate the effect size of any change or improvement

---

Effect Size

The measure of the strength of the relationship between two variables (Fergeson, 2009). For a program evaluation, the size of the improvement attributed to the program.

Table C.6
Program Responses for Item 14

Response	Description	Example
Effective (Moderate to Large Improvement)	• Compared to nonparticipants, those in the program demonstrated an improvement in the outcome, and the improvement was moderate to large and/or clinically meaningful. • After participation in the program, participants demonstrated an improvement in the outcome, and the improvement was moderate to large and/or clinically meaningful.	After participation in the program, 50 percent of participants no longer meet diagnostic criteria for posttraumatic stress disorder.
Effective (Small Improvement)	• Compared to nonparticipants, those in the program demonstrated an improvement in the outcome, but the improvement was small and/or not clinically meaningful. • After participation in the program, participants demonstrated an improvement in the outcome, but the improvement was small and/or not clinically meaningful.	After participation in the program, marital satisfaction increases somewhat, but divorce rates remain largely unchanged and marital satisfaction remains low overall.
Not Effective	• Compared to nonparticipants, those in the program had similar outcomes. • After participation in the program, there was no change in the outcome of interest.	Suicide rates remain unchanged after administration of a suicide prevention program.
Harmful	• Compared to nonparticipants, those in the program had worse outcomes. • Participants performed more poorly after they finished the program than before they began.	After participation in the program, posttraumatic stress symptomatology increases.

attributed to the program. Note that the reviewer's estimate of effect size (from small to large) provides the opportunity to note the clinical significance of any statistically significant finding.

BACKGROUND (Item 14)

The goal of a program evaluation is to provide decisionmakers with information about whether a program was harmful, ineffective, or helpful (McDavid and Hawthorn, 2006). However, when a program is helpful, it is also necessary to understand the *effect size*. Typically, decisionmakers are interested not only in whether a program is associated with an improvement in functioning, but also how much of an improvement is observed. Small effect sizes are improvements that can be documented with a statistical test, but that would be difficult to observe with the "naked eye" (Cohen, 1992). Moderate and large effect sizes are statistically significant AND could be observed with the "naked eye" by a careful observer (Cohen, 1992).

Section III: Population Priority
ITEM 15. Consider the population served by the program. Rate the extent to which the population is a current, exceptionally high priority population to the DoD. Consider the extent to which the population served by the program is a sufficiently high priority such that it could conceivably change the expansion recommendation for the program.

Is the POPULATION PRIORITY high?

      Yes   No

INSTRUCTIONS (Item 15)

The priority of the population captures a number of considerations, including whether there is an identified need or gap in services for a particular population, whether participants have a rare condition or experience, and whether participant outcomes are directly tied to operational success, among others. Given that the population priorities can change over time, please provide your assessment based on information provided by the program and your knowledge of the current environment. Provide the rationale for your selection in the space provided in the rating box.

Although all service members are highly valued and can be considered to be a priority population, this criterion will have little usefulness if the majority of programs are rated as such. Rather, this criterion is designed to capture programs serving a population of *exceptionally* high priority. Based on the decision tree (see Figure 2.1 in Chapter Two), when a population is deemed a high priority, decisionmakers may accept a lesser-quality program evaluation or program for dissemination. Decisionmakers should be certain that a program is designed for a population with a significant unmet need or a population that has been explicitly mandated to receive services through a binding policy recommendation prior to providing a high rating. **It is expected that only a very small number of populations will be rated with a high priority.**

BACKGROUND (Item 15)

Although the empirical evidence provides important information about the success of a program, any decisionmaking body or decisionmaker will need to consider additional factors beyond program outcome. One such factor is the priority of the population served by the program. Population priorities will shift over time, and thus are impossible to document in a static decision tool. This item relies explicitly on the expertise of the reviewer to make a judgment about whether the social and political context exerts significant pressure on program recommendations at the time any decisions regarding program expansion are being made.

Section IV: Policy Priority

16. Consider the political and social factors that will influence decisionmaking about the program and rate the extent to which those factors associated with the program are sufficiently strong that they could conceivably change the expansion recommendation for the program.

Is the POLICY PRIORITY high?

      Yes   No

INSTRUCTIONS (Item 16)

The policy context of a program includes a range of factors such as congressional or military mandates, current military actions and deployment cycles, community-level or national support for the program or the issue it is addressing, and civilian or military reports or recommendations related to psychological health or TBI. Given that policy priorities can change over time, please provide your assessment of the policy priority based on information provided by the program and your knowledge of the current environment. Provide the rationale for your selection in the space provided.

BACKGROUND (Item 16)

Although the empirical evidence provides important information about the success of a program, any decisionmaking body or decisionmaker will need to consider additional factors beyond program outcomes. One such factor is the social and political context in which the program operates, and the resulting DoD policy priorities. This context will shift over time and is thus impossible to document in a static decision tool. This item relies explicitly on the expertise of the reviewer to make a judgment about whether social and political priorities exert significant pressure on program recommendations at the time any decisions regarding program expansion are being made.

References

Acosta JD, Gonzalez GC, Gillen EM, Garnett J, Farmer CM, and Weinick RM. *The Development and Application of the RAND Program Classification Tool: The RAND Toolkit, Volume 1.* Santa Monica, CA: RAND Corporation, RR-487/1-OSD, 2014. As of January 2014:
http://www.rand.org/pubs/research_reports/RR487z1.html

Acosta JD, Reynolds KA, Gillen EM, Feeney K, Farmer CM, and Weinick, RM. *The RAND Online Repository of Measures for Evaluating Psychological Health and TBI Programs: The RAND Toolkit, Volume 2.* Santa Monica, CA: RAND Corporation, RR-487/2-OSD, 2014. As of January 2014:
http://www.rand.org/pubs/research_reports/RR487z2.html

Basham RB. "Scientific and Practical Advantages of Comparative Design in Psychotherapy Outcome Research." *Journal of Consulting and Clinical Psychology*, Vol. 54, No. 1, 1986, pp. 88–94.

Beckett M, Hawken A, and Jacknowitz A. *Accountability for After-School Care: Devising Standards and Measuring Adherence to Them.* Santa Monica, CA: RAND Corporation, MR-1411-SSCCP, 2001. As of November 2013:
http://www.rand.org/pubs/monograph_reports/MR1411.html

Bordens KS, and Abbott BB. *Research Design and Methods: A Process Approach*, 3rd ed., Mountain View, CA: Mayfield, 1996.

Botvin GJ. *From Research to Policy: Advancing Prevention Science and Practice.* Presidential address presented at the 11th annual meeting of the Society for Prevention Research, Washington, D.C., 2003.

Cohen J. "A Power Primer." *Psychological Bulletin*, Vol. 112, No. 1, 1992, pp. 155–159.

Cohen RJ, and Swerdlik M. *Psychological Testing and Assessment.* New York: McGraw-Hill, 2002.

Deeks JJ, Dinnes J, D'Amico R, Sowden AJ, Sakarovitch C, Song F, Petticrew M, and Altman DG. "Evaluating Non-Randomized Intervention Studies." *Health Technology Assessment*, Vol. 7, No. 27, 2003, pp. 1–186.

Fergeson CJ. "An Effect Size Primer. A Guide for Clinicians and Researchers." *Professional Psychology: Research and Practice*, Vol. 40, No. 5, 2009, pp. 532–538.

Fisher LD, Dixon DO, Herson J, Frankowski RF, Hearron MS, and Peace KE, "Intention to Treat in Clinical Trials." In KE Peace, ed., *Statistical Issues in Drug Research and Development*, New York: Marcel Dekker, 1990, pp. 331–350.

Hartman JM, Forsen JW, Wallace MS, and Neely JG. "Tutorials in Clinical Research: Part IV: Recognizing and Controlling Bias." *The Laryngoscope*, Vol. 112, No. 1, 2002, pp. 23–31.

Katrak P, Bialocerkowski AE, Massy-Westropp N, Kumar S, and Grimmer KA. "A Systematic Review of the Content of Critical Appraisal Tools." *BMC Medical Research Methodology*, Vol. 4, 2004, pp. 1–11.

McDavid JC, and Hawthorn LRL. *Program Evaluation and Performance Measurement.* Thousand Oaks, CA: Sage Publications, 2006.

Norton WE, and Mittman BS. *Scaling-Up Health Promotion/Disease Prevention Programs in Community Settings: Barriers, Facilitators, and Initial Recommendations.* The Patrick and Catherine Weldon Donaghue Medical Research Foundation, 2010.

Oakes JM, and Kaufman JS. *Methods in Social Epidemiology.* San Francisco: Jossey-Bass, 2006.

Ryan G, Farmer CM, Adamson D, and Weinick RM. *A Program Manager's Guide to Program Improvement in Ongoing Psychological Health and Traumatic Brain Injury Programs: The RAND Toolkit, Volume 4.* Santa Monica, CA: RAND Corporation, RR-487/4-OSD, 2014. As of January 2014:
http://www.rand.org/pubs/research_reports/RR487z4.html

Thomas BH, Ciliska D, Dobbins M, and Micucci S. "A Process for Systematically Reviewing the Literature: Providing the Research Evidence for Public Health Nursing Interventions." *Worldviews on Evidence-Based Nursing,* Vol. 3, 2004, pp. 176-184.

U.S. Code of Federal Regulations, Title 45. Department of Health and Human Services, National Institutes of Health, Office for Protection from Research Risks, Part 46, Protection of Human Subjects. January 15, 2009. As of May 15, 2013:
http://www.hhs.gov/ohrp/humansubjects/guidance/45cfr46.html

Weinick RM, Beckjord EB, Farmer CM, Martin LM, Gillen EM, Acosta JD, Fisher MP, Garnett J, Gonzalez GC, Helmus TC, Jaycox LH, Reynolds KA, Salcedo N, and Scharf DM. *Programs Addressing Psychological Health and Traumatic Brain Injury Among U.S. Military Servicemembers and Their Families.* Santa Monica, CA: RAND Corporation, TR-950-OSD, 2011. As of January 6, 2012:
http://www.rand.org/pubs/technical_reports/TR950.html

West S, King V, Carey TS, Lohr KN, McKoy N, Sutton SF, and Lux L. *Systems to Rate the Strength of Scientific Evidence.* Rockville, MD: Agency for Healthcare Research and Quality, 2002.

Zaza S, Wright-De Agüero LK, Briss PA, Truman BI, Hopkins DP, Hennessy MH, Sosin DM, Anderson L, Carande-Kulis VG, Teutsch SM, and Pappaioanou VG. "Data Collection Instrument and Procedure for Systematic Reviews in the Guide to Community Prevention Services." *American Journal of Preventative Medicine,* Vol. 18, 2000, pp. 44–74.